SACRED FIRE

Northern Testimonies

The McGill Family

...God anointed Jesus of Nazareth with the Holy Ghost and with power: who went about doing good, and healing all that were oppressed of the devil; for God was with him.

Acts 10:38.

SACRED FIRE: NORTHERN TESTIMONIES

First Edition

Cover Painted by: Sonja McGill

ISBN 978-1-0690288-0-8

ALL SCRIPTURE IS TAKEN FROM
THE KING JAMES VERSION OF THE HOLY BIBLE.

 This book is a work of nonfiction based on the author's personal experiences. However, to protect the privacy and anonymity of certain individuals, some names and identifying details have been changed. Any resemblance to persons, living or deceased, beyond those described is purely coincidental.

Contact the publisher through www.iamtheway.ca.

TABLE OF CONTENTS

FOREWORD

We are living in one of the most exciting and significant times in history. The opportunity for the body of Christ to bring the light of the gospel into the darkness is more urgent than ever. If the harvest was ready 2,000 years ago when Jesus called His disciples to lift up their eyes to the fields, how much more ready is it today?

The ministry of Jesus described in Acts 10:38 is a key aspect of most everything we do: "How God anointed Jesus of Nazareth with the Holy Ghost and with power, who went about doing good and healing all who were oppressed of the devil, for God was with him." This verse reminds us that Jesus' mission was to bring freedom, healing, and hope to those in bondage—and it is the same mission for us today. For Jesus plainly declares it to be so in John 20:21. "...as my Father hath sent me, even so send I you." Similarly, in John 14:12, where he says, "He that believeth on me, the works that I do shall he do also..." And again, in Luke 6:40, he states that the disciple shall be as his master.

The church is not starting some new form of ministry. It is simply continuing the ministry of Jesus Christ to the world—though now with the benefit of understanding the scope of the death, burial, and resurrection and the amazing mystery of Christ in us.

Jesus came to show us how to walk as sons and daughters of God. Ephesians 5:1, 5:8. Is that not what was lost? When man fell, God lost his family. But Jesus came to restore it. Why else would a new birth be part of the plan of salvation? It is time to call people back home to the Father's house.

For those who are bold in their faith and fully committed to God, countless opportunities will arise to witness His life and power at work. Whether through preaching the gospel, laying hands on the sick, casting out devils, or watching Jesus triumph in seemingly hopeless situations—God's will can be done through our simple obedience, just as it was through Jesus.

Many of you who know us have heard the stories in this book firsthand. Some have met the people involved; others have even traveled with us and seen the power of Jesus at work. For those who haven't, we present these pages as a testimony of a living Jesus, still bringing healing, deliverance, and freedom—just as He did when He walked the earth.

One scripture that resonates deeply with us is Revelation 12:11, where we are shown how the saints overcame the enemy:

- By the blood of the Lamb
- By the word of their testimony
- By not loving their lives unto death

This book is the word of our testimony—not about how broken we were before meeting Jesus, but about how powerful and faithful He is after we met Him. Salvation is just the beginning of a lifelong journey of walking with the King of Kings and seeing His power manifest through us.

The accounts you'll read are firsthand stories from our journals, often recorded the day the events took place. We've shared these experiences to encourage the body of Christ. These are not comprehensive insights into First Nations or mission work—many others have made significant contributions in those areas. This is simply a little bit of our story.

We haven't sugarcoated the challenges. As Paul writes in 2 Corinthians 1:8, intense situations remind us how desperately we need God's mercy and grace. There are moments when you don't fully understand what you're facing, and it is only by His strength that you move forward.

Each person we meet in this book is on their own journey, and we don't always see the end of every story. But as Paul says in 1 Corinthians 3:6, some plant, some water, but it is God who gives the increase. There have been times when we've reaped the harvest, witnessing souls saved or bodies healed, and other times when we've only been able to plant or water seeds. Even so, we have learned to never underestimate the power of just a single word of encouragement—those seeds go deeper than you might imagine.

As we've worked alongside First Nations communities, we've come to believe that God is preparing them to be used for a great harvest of souls in Canada and the United States. It has been an incredible honour to serve alongside our First Nations brothers and sisters, casting the Kingdom's nets into the world in hopes of saving some. But we really haven't seen anything yet! The time of the final harvest is now, but there remains a great need for more workers.

If you've ever wondered, "Can I truly trust God and see him move like He did in the Bible?" I believe this book will help answer that question. The same Jesus who went about doing good and healing the oppressed is still working today through his people. Yes, you can trust him. Yes, you will see his power move.

Wherever darkness prevails, Jesus desires his light to shine. No devil, sickness, or oppression is too great to be overcome by raw faith and a bold heart. You will face challenges, but as 2 Corinthians 2:14 declares, God will always cause you to triumph!

May you be encouraged by these stories of what Jesus is doing today, in Canada and around the world.

INTRODUCTION

This book explores situations and challenges faced by various First Nations communities, making it essential to begin with some historical background. In Canada, an insidious and destructive system targeted the Indigenous peoples, known as the *residential school system*. Operated by the Canadian government in collaboration with several mainstream churches—Roman Catholic, Anglican, Methodist, Presbyterian, and United—this system ran from 1831 until as recently as 1996. Although its stated purpose was to educate and convert Indigenous children, its legacy is one of profound abuse, pain, and communal trauma.

The impact of these schools cannot be understated. For over 100 years, Indigenous children suffered emotional, psychological, sexual, and spiritual abuse within these institutions. Many of these abuses were carried out under the guise of faith. As Paul warns in 2 Corinthians 11:26, there were "false brethren" in his time—people pretending to serve Christ but working against His true purpose and serving the devil.

Similarly, many of those involved in these schools acted in the name of Christianity but served a different agenda. Paul's description of such people as "false apostles, deceitful workers" (2 Corinthians 11:13) resonates deeply when we consider the harm done.

Only through the healing power of Christ can restoration begin for those affected by this devastation.

To illustrate the gravity of what was organized against the First Nations, here are two personal accounts shared by survivors as they were told to us directly:

One woman, part of what was called the "60s scoop," recounted how, as a child, she and her brother were playing on their reserve when a government agent arrived in a floatplane. Her mother had just gone to the store to get some milk when he appeared at the edge of their property. Enticed by his offer to see the plane, they were taken away without warning and placed in foster care, severed from their family and culture. She never saw her mother again.

Another woman shared how her sister was taken during a gathering in their community. While the adults were at a meeting held by the Catholic

Church, officials swept through the town, rounding up children and transporting them by boat to St. Anne's Residential School. Her parents, desperate to get her back, paddled two hundred kilometres down the western edge of James Bay to the school. Against the odds, they managed to reunite with their daughter and return home, paddling the 200 km north—an exceptionally rare escape.

Three young boys from the same school would not be as successful, disappearing into the northern wilderness in an escape attempt, never to return home. The school simply reports their deaths as "*drowned?*"

These stories reflect only a fraction of the evil that took place within the residential school system, yet they paint a vivid picture of the long-lasting effects. Communities were shattered, families were torn apart, and a deep mistrust of the government and the church was seeded.

One of the contributors to the residential school reports for the Cree, who served as my translator during several evenings of preaching in 2018, shared a personal insight: "We lost the ability to parent." Could this have been the core purpose of the devil's attack on the First Nations people at that time? This devastating consequence of the schools' efforts to strip Indigenous children of their identity and culture is a key part of the legacy left behind. As Matthew Coon Come, the Grand Chief of the James Bay Cree at the time, stated in an interview with CBC, these actions were far more than "cultural genocide... it was a criminal offence."

While the impacts of this system were unevenly felt across different communities, the ripples of trauma continue to affect many to this day. Nevertheless, there are shining examples of resilience—communities where the fabric of family and culture remains strong. As we engage with these stories, it is crucial to listen and approach each individual with respect, never assuming their experience but being mindful of the potential scars left behind.

The generational effects of trauma can be profound, as cycles of pain and loss continue unless broken. Proverbs 22:6 reminds us of the power of formative experiences: "Train up a child in the way he should go; when he is old, he will not depart from it." The residential schools trained children in cruelty and detachment, leaving many trapped in a cycle of abuse. But hope remains, for healing is possible through Christ.

In Indigenous cultures, identity is often deeply tied to the community. It has been our great joy to discover places where this sense of belonging remains intact, a testament to the incredible resilience of the First Nations people. This communal strength was undoubtedly a target of the enemy, for no culture on earth is immune to attacks against the family. Some are just more obvious.

It's essential to acknowledge that for many Indigenous people, the name of Jesus carries a heavy stigma because of the trauma inflicted under His banner by false believers. Yet, we have found that when the true Spirit of the Lord is present, healing and reconciliation are possible. The gospel is indeed good news for all nations, and we must carry it forward with humility and love.

As we proceed, let us remember the light that shines in the darkness (John 1:5). No matter how deep the wounds, Christ's healing hand can restore, and His love can triumph over any darkness.

For I, saith the Lord, will be unto her a wall of fire round about, and will be the glory in the midst of her.

Zechariah 2:5

Chapter One

Things to Come

The elder, who had come rushing in late to service, was extremely excited. I have met the Cree people in many places across Canada. Those I have known have a wonderful balance between being stoic in nature, which feels ancient and rich in its depth, and a wonderful lightheartedness, which flows like a river of joy that seems to come straight from their hearts.

Many of our Cree friends have a remarkable ability to find a laugh in even the hardest of times, but it was rare for me to see a continuous bubbling excitement that wouldn't let up.

The translator for the night was a pastor named Daniel. The elder was speaking to him rapidly in Cree, and he was translating for me.

"She says they weren't coming to church, but then her daughter went outside and heard angels singing in the sky above the church. She called to her, and she came out and also heard the angels singing over where the church was," Daniel told me.

What a thought! An angelic choir, just hovering over our heads while we're worshipping the Lord in this old, dilapidated building with rusted mesh grates screwed into the siding, doing their best to protect the windows. There were no cozy chairs or fancy pews. You had to sit on old wooden benches, originally made for a makeshift movie theatre thirty years prior, which had long since vanished. The ceiling was partly collapsing. There was a rickety little stage, an old drum kit, and something of a pulpit. It brought to mind John 1:46: Can anything good come out of Nazareth? And truly, the answer was ironically the same: "Come and see."

As they were on their porch listening to the angels sing, a pickup truck pulled up, and the man driving it yelled to the women, "Do you want to go to church?!" "Yes!" they both replied and headed for the truck. Who wouldn't want to go to church when angels are singing over it?

The services had no time limit. We would simply begin when there were enough folks or musicians to start and then stop when the Holy Ghost seemed to be done with what He wanted to do that night. It was the first time I had preached five nights a week for multiple weeks. We were pressing in, and God was answering.

Many of those nights were like living in a dream. I'd often heard of old-time revivals, but now my eyes were seeing. Seeing how the Holy Spirit would reach out and touch various ones. Sometimes He would draw them in from the street, even the other side of town. It was a constant cycle of divine appointments and demonstrations of the mighty power of God.

I hadn't initially been expecting to preach for five nights a week, but Daniel, a wonderfully warm-hearted and kind man, whom God had sent up one month before us to prepare the church, met me the morning of the second day after we had arrived.

He said, "You'll preach tonight." I said, "Okay." And so I did. After he heard me preach, he said, "You'll preach all week now." And so I did.

This rolled on, week after week, the Lord saving, healing, and delivering in a northern, fly-in only, First Nations community called Attawapiskat.

You felt like you were always walking on holy ground. There was a fire, and it was sacred. I felt like I couldn't be more in the centre of God's will. This wasn't just the bullseye. It was the middle of the bullseye. It was the heart of the gospel being lived out—going to the highways and byways—inviting anyone who would listen to the call to the wedding feast! Proclaiming the great saving and healing gospel of Jesus Christ. And the Lord, as stated in Mark 16, worked with us and confirmed the word with signs following.

One evening, God invaded the church with such awesome power that it left the pastor and me hiding up against the wall. I had barely finished preaching the message when the Holy Spirit fell on the people. I didn't need to give an altar call, as one by one they came forward, weeping under the power of the Spirit. I had never seen such a thing. The weight was tangible.

One elderly lady came forward very solemnly and then, all of a sudden, burst out in laughter. And in an instant, without anyone touching her, we watched her get thrown into the side wall of the church, down over onto a pew, and then spun down onto the floor.

After I saw that, I got off the stage as fast as I could and tucked into the side of the church, burying myself in the wall. The people came forward and wept. Everyone in the place was enveloped in God.

Daniel asked me, "Should we pray for them?"

"No!" I replied. "Don't touch them! God is doing it Himself!"

It was an awesome night. The invasion of Heaven, bombarding the souls of men and women with his mighty healing power. Changing hearts and minds in a moment. Taking brokenness and repairing it with such perfect ease. It was truly the work of the Lord. No man had a hand in it. He alone got the glory.

We had been there two years prior, during the suicide crisis, when God opened a door to bring us in. But before we get into that, I should really start at the beginning.

Chapter Two

In the Beginning

When you're seven and your best friend is going away with his family to be missionaries in Papua New Guinea, you get impressed with a certain kind of Christianity that never leaves you. There were still headhunter tribes active at that time, and yet off they went, children and all.

It seems the real Christian is built for just that—going into the darkest of the dark with an unquenchable fire. A fearlessness. A bold desire to face peril for the sake of bringing a message from the Great King of Heaven and Earth. A message of good news. News that takes one from the mud pit to the palace.

I was fortunate with how I was brought up. When I was younger, there was always an element of the supernatural around: the potential of God doing God things. Even those family friends in PNG had miraculous stories of imminent danger (being chased by a tribe that wanted to kill them) and the deliverance from it by the ones God gives charge over us to keep us in all our ways (a band of glowing angels appeared on a hill and scared the would-be murderer's away).

What's a kid supposed to do with that sort of information? You can't ignore it. It's either real or it's not real. And if it's real, that demands a response—an investigation.

Our family was far from perfect, and we would have struggles at times, as all do, learning and growing, but there would be wonderful realities of Heaven's care: Food being delivered to our door, and no footprints left in the snow. Money to pay a mortgage bill slipped through the slot in the door as my mom prayed. It was just what was needed, and no one but Heaven knew.

One day I needed lunch for school, but we didn't have any bread. As my mom was driving me to school, there in the middle of the road was a loaf of bread. It was Bambie bread. My mom pulled the car over, grabbed the bread (it was still warm), dropped me off, and by lunch delivered my sandwich. Psalm 37:25.

My dad had driven the car with an empty fuel tank on multiple occasions over great distances while going to or coming from Christian events. There was even a time when our empty heating oil tank kept producing heat for us when it was also a long time empty. Supernatural oil provision isn't just for the Old Testament.

There was divine protection by the bushel: being saved from car crashes. Oh, how good it is when the Lord is our shield! I fell out of the top of a tree once. But instead of falling straight down, I floated down at a 45-degree angle so I would miss the swingset directly under me. My brothers saw this and would call me Superman for a while after. When I started to fall, everything went white, and the next thing I knew, I was on my feet on the ground, looking high up to where I was. So many wonderful things happened that taught me that there was another world we could engage with. There was actually a God.

But how do we fully know this God? We pray, yes. We read his word. But God has also set certain ones in the body—His gifts to the church, as Ephesians 4:11 says. They are to equip and strengthen the body of Christ! They are here to help us down the road.

One time, one of those gifts came to stay at our house. He had come up from America. He arrived with nothing but a grocery bag filled with a couple of changes of clothes, a heart full of the word, and a soul brimming with the Holy Ghost. Some called him an Apostle. I knew him as a Texan. He came to visit with my parents. It was around 1982. There was no social media. No texting. And no one else knew, or so we thought.

But one night, as brother Robert, as he was called, was preparing to teach, there was a knock at the door. Someone asked for him by name and if he was in this house.

"Yes...but how?"

"I was praying and was told he would be here."

Soon the door was being knocked on every few minutes. People had been told through prayer, visions, and dreams to come to our house on this night. Some even came from the States, driving hundreds of miles. And no one knew us or that he was there.

There would be a packed house before the night was through, everyone there to be taught the word of God, and all led miraculously by the Spirit.

That sort of thing makes an impression: the value God places on the teaching of his word without the trappings of the doctrines of men or devils.

It is this appreciation for the word that would get implanted in me as a young boy. And the working out of it would be a major key to the victory we would see when called to the First Nations. If God has exalted his word above his name, how important must that word be?! Psalm 138:2.

Chapter Three

Maps

When Shannon and I were married in May of 2001, we went on our honeymoon to Europe. A very classic thing to do for our generation. We flew into Vienna and were flying out of Paris two months later with no plans in between but what the Lord would have us do. It was a crash course in learning how to be led by the Spirit as a couple. And we saw his wonderful provision and guidance, his specific care for us, in even the smallest of things.

One time, while in Paris, we didn't know where we were, and so we prayed, "Oh God, if we could have a map." And then we turned the corner, and there, on a little grass embankment, just a few feet from our prayer, was a map of Paris. (I still have that map.) God leads. God guides. And when you get lost, he can give you a map.

Even the provision on our trip was miraculously sustained. Each time we'd need funds, it would be in our account. We arrived back in Canada with a couple

Austrian shillings, the very last of our funds having taken care of our final train ride to the Paris airport. It was a genuine Luke 10:4 experience.

But what has been the greatest map we've ever received from him is truly his wonderful word. What a thing for man to have. A divine book in which one can drink when thirsty, eat when hungry, receive comfort when troubled, have vision when clouded, and find direct purpose when wondering.

What I have learned is that the Great Map always leads along the best route. It wants us to walk on the King's Road. This road is paved with his words, which he has laid out in His word, and has always proven to be the highest form of life I've tasted.

It is always the more excellent way when we follow closely to Christ. When we see his example of selfless yet powerful love. See His way of elevating what people thought could never shine. There is a secret in that way of walking: when that is the primary way, and not just an occasional place one visits when they feel convicted.

In 2008, we had been married for seven years. It was a hard year, but those often exist when God is trying to squeeze you into something specific. I was out for one of those "what do I do now" prayer walks and wandered into the local Christian bookstore. I was leafing through the "classics" section and came across *The Cross and the Switchblade.* I had never read it, though I was somewhat familiar with Wilkerson and his work in New York. I had just enough to purchase the book, and so I did. Another one for our bookshelf filled with stories of "Great Christians That I Wish I Knew."

I think many hungry Pentecostal-type people have a similar shelf. Ours consists of sermons and accounts of John Lake, Smith Wigglesworth, Mother Etter, Evan Roberts, and Rees Howells. Some tales from Azusa Street and the Hebrides revivals. And on and on... *Like a Mighty Wind* by Mel Tari, *Visions Beyond the Veil* by H.A. Baker. Pullinger's eye opening and fearless, *Chasing the Dragon.* A sprinkling of Watchman Nee and the gut wrenching book, *Lilies Amongst Thorns*, a riveting account of the underground church in China, coupled with *The Heavenly Man* by Brother Yun. And then, of course, *God's Smuggler* by Brother Andrew, who also walked in the Royal Way.

In the healing works, some Bosworth, T.L. Osborne, and Curry Blake (who's DHT course should be mandatory these days for anyone who cares to see people healed and set free.) There are so many others as well: Lester Sumrall, A.A. Allen, Andrew Wommack, Norval Hayes, Charles Spurgeon, Andrew Murray, Reinhardt Bonke, G.C. Bevington, the Bakers, Supresa Sithole, and others.

If there are souls being saved in great power, we need to know about it. What was it about Finney, Wesley, and Booth that made them what they were? They had a determination that others seemed to lack. A grit and courage that was rare indeed. A focus that was singular: souls must be saved!

These sorts of books usually do one of two things to their readers: provoke you to love and good works, or make you question where you go to church and what on earth the pastor has been teaching you all this time.

The genuine believer wants to live where lives aren't just "touched" but are changed! And you will never be satisfied until you are there—where devils are challenged and evicted, diseases shrink back in terror at the healing river of the Spirit, and souls are saved from destruction through the preaching of the death, burial, and resurrection of Christ! The preaching of the cross is not without power today! And testimonies shouldn't be solely reserved for foreign missions. Miracles don't need to see your passport stamp before they manifest for you. They should be part of the daily lives of those that walk with a living Jesus.

I was also challenged to reach for that high call. Especially as I had met people like those I read about in our books, and I couldn't just dismiss the potentiality of such a walk as fiction! One fellow our family knew rather well was supernaturally flown to northern Russia and ended up in a cabin in the woods where pastors had been gathering, all led there by the Spirit, because God said he was sending his servant there to teach them. I met that man.

I also met a man who was led out of Romania (while it was under communism) by a pillar of light. He and two other pastors were led past the border guards and the dogs and the guns, totally unnoticed. He crossed from East to West Germany on a train with no papers. The guard came into the traincar and asked for everyone's papers but his. The guard didn't even see him. I met that man. His name is Ilie Caroma. He went to Heaven recently, having finished his race. But I shook his hand. I stood in his house in St. Louis. I know he was real and not just in some book on a shelf.

I'd seen things as a child. Wonderful things. Biblical things, made real. And now here Shannon and I were, seven years into marriage, and still trying our best to machete our way through the vines of this world into the Kingdom. But you must become like a child. You must learn to depend fully on God and not just what you know about him. It is a simple path, but it requires the sort of map only a childlike heart can see. Matthew 18:3. Paul tells us not to be moved away from the simplicity that is in Christ. 2 Corinthians 11:3.

There was a vision given to a missionary of the present day, David Hogan, who works deep in the mountain jungles of Mexico. He saw a field. In that field, he saw a present. It was a large box wrapped with a bow. In that field was a bull, and the bull wanted what was in the box. And so the bull tried with all of his strength to open that box, but he couldn't. Then a baby appeared. And with the simplest of ease, the baby pulled off the ribbon and, with joy, opened the box.

David understood the message. He had been trying in his own strength to get God's power. To get God to move. He changed his prayer. He said, "Make me like that baby!" Nothing receives like a child's heart. Dependency is key.

It's so very true that God has to bring us back to a simple place before he can really use us. Much of our own efforts get in the way and never accomplish what we want them to anyway. This modern life entangles one like no other age has. Paul is explicit in his charge to Timothy in 2 Timothy 2:4 that a soldier isn't to get entangled in the affairs of life. This is the reason many Christians have a hard time in their warfare. They are split between two kingdoms. Power follows intention. If your heart is split, your intention is split, and the power of God cannot flow as it should.

Near the beginning of 2008, life for us started to turn back towards simplicity. That usually means branches in your life start getting pruned! (When a vinedresser prunes, 90% of the previous year's wood is cut back.) And so we were cut back to a little more than our roots and main stock, but then the momentum of Heaven began rolling through our lives. We could tell the predestined good works were calling.

Things started to ramp up that February, when a curious thing was discovered as I started reading to Shannon from what I had purchased earlier that day, *The Cross and the Switchblade*. David Wilkerson made a comment a few pages in about when things changed for him. He said it was when he got rid of his TV. And he said the date. It was February 9, 1958. And then I realized what day it was: February 9, 2008. It was fifty years later, to the very day. Surely God was up to something.

Now, of course, we can walk with Jesus every day and just obey the word and see wonderful results. Like William Booth said, "I'm not waiting for a move of God; I am a move of God." It's true. Jesus sent the Christian to be everything most people are praying for God to send. So we don't need to go hunting for prophetic unctions under every rock or in each church service; however, our Father does think about us a lot (Psalm 139:17-18, Jeremiah 29:11), and if the Bible shows us anything, it is that God involves Himself directly and powerfully in the life of the one whose heart is perfect toward him. 2 Chronicles 16:9.

The following day, Sunday, I was getting ready to go to church, still musing on the fifty years to the day "coincidence." Shannon and I had some of our honeymoon photos out, and our one daughter, Alaya, was pointing at one of me.

I was in Austria, sitting on a wooden fence with mountains rolling up behind me. "Look, dad, you're sitting on a fence!" Alaya said.

"Hmmm," I mused.

And off I went to church.

The service was moving along like normal. Nothing felt different. But then there was a brief moment, just at the end of worship, where God decided to press down a little bit. Now, I didn't see who said it, as I was at the back, but someone lifted up their voice in the stillness and said, "The Lord says, 'Stop sitting on the fence! Will you or won't you go?!'"

Well now, what do you say to that? I didn't know if that was for anyone else, but I sure knew it was for me. I went home and thought about where the 'go' was. I have since learned that much of the go is in the willingness to go. Like God said to Rees Howells, "Are you willing to be made willing?"

Often, we just need to be willing to go, and then God starts to direct. I have never seen direction given when I've waited for everything to be in place before I had a willingness to go, and very often, it comes when we've put the vehicle of life in gear, having taken it out of neutral. Once the motion aspect of faith is engaged, He quickly brings about what needs to happen for the path to be clear.

Faith is always ready to run, as it's based on the clear promises in the word of God. It's based on what is. It's based on what God has already said. It's not presumptuous. If God has said, *I'll do such and such*, he will indeed do such and such, and you don't need to pray about *whether* he will; just recognize he has already promised to. In fact, to pray in a wondering way about something God has already commanded, given, or said He would do is quite the insult to the Captain of our soul!

Very often in the word, God gives object lessons in nature to help our stubborn heads get the point of what he's trying to say. For example, the Bible shows us the word is like seed, bread, meat, or light. He uses thunder to help us understand the strength of his glory and the power of His voice. Psalm 29:3-4. So when God wants to get your attention, he can.

One night, there was the sound of a large explosion and a brilliant flash of light just outside our house. It sounded like a keg of dynamite going off. Shannon was in the bedroom and grabbed the baby to run for cover. My brother, who was visiting with us, came outside with me to investigate. There was nothing physical that we could see. A couple days after this, Shannon would be given an open vision.

I had been praying in the front room and was being mightily blessed by the presence of the Lord, so much so that I told Shannon that she just had to go in there and at least sit down on the chair I was praying in. Even if it was for just a little while. She did, and in a short time Hebrew letters appeared to her on the computer screen. However, this computer was off, and the screen was black. She wrote the letters down, and when we looked the word up, it was the Hebrew word for *Rachel.*

One of the greatest prophetic verses about Rachel is in Jeremiah 31:15, where we see her weeping over the loss of her children—the destruction of the young. Little did we know that we were only a few months away from our first steps into the world of First Nations ministry, and if there is a land where the mother's weep for their children, that is the one.

Not long after this, we were impressed that we would be going west. But into what, we weren't certain. But then one day, Shannon, while in prayer, was told we would be working with First Nations. That was a new idea for us. We had done various things in ministry prior but had never had a focus on any particular group. We had no idea what that meant.

Naturally, I knew that there were First Nations. We learned a little about them in school. Shannon was born in Brantford, the land of the Six Nations, and had gone to school with them. She had been given a small tour of the First Nation's church, Mohawk Chapel, when she was a teenager. And I had once worked with a native guy named Henry. Aside from that, it was *Dances with Wolves, Northern Exposure,* and *Dance Me Outside* that formed the sum of our knowledge concerning First Nations at that time. But it was something God was leading into, so you just say, "Yes, Lord," and follow the map!

Chapter Four

New Horizon

So how does one "work" with First Nations? We weren't a ministry. We were just a little family. Well, it went like this: There was a couple that my parents met when I was young—Bruce and Carmina Thomson. I had visited them a few years prior, travelling with them while they preached and sang through the southern United States. They had done radical things with YWAM behind the Iron Curtain. They were the only people I knew that were west.

So I contacted them to let them know that the Lord was leading us west, and if we could, might we land wherever they are and continue seeking God from there? They said they would pray about it and let us know. A couple days later, they got back to us. They said the Lord impressed them to have us come and that they had a place we would be able to stay.

"And by the way, we're running a First Nations youth camp. If you'd like to help with that while you're with us." – God knows his business.

In the summer of 2008, we landed in Edmonton, Alberta. Carmina picked us up at the airport and drove us down to where they were, near Drayton Valley.

We stayed in a Hillbillies mansion: a converted school bus with no washroom (that was the outhouse in the woods) and no running water (that was the hose by the well) with our two young daughters, in the middle of bear and cougar country. We would spend that summer getting introduced to the world of Canada's First Nations through a group called *Camp Living Water*. Larry Keegstra was the director. He also ran the British Columbia sister camp near Vanderhoof.

It was a time when there were a lot of gang wars on the reservations in Alberta. *The Cross and the Switchblade* was certainly a fitting primer. The police came to the camp one day to interview one of the girls (I believe she was about ten), as she had been the main witness to a shooting just before coming to camp. That became a normal story we would hear during this time.

As for the camp, it was really a "camp" last. It was a resort for some. An escape for others. A respite from madness. A safe place. A window into a new potential reality where Jesus can calm the raging sea of life. Though there were camp-like activities during the day, there was a wonderful grittiness and realness to the ministry there, and you needed to be shockproof.

There was always talk of spirits. Some were coming and carrying children away. Some stories are too wild to put in this book. But there was also a great amount of grief and sadness, fear and pain, and then the loss... the endless loss. So many mother's and father's and brother's and sister's... gone. Gone to drugs, accidents, or violence... or just gone... missing... wandered off somewhere or snatched up in some evil scheme.

It was like a door had opened up, and I was looking into a place where the devil was able to work unchecked. Unchallenged. I had never heard such stories of loss. But even in the midst of all this, these kids, who came from all over the province, would have the most wonderful encounters with Jesus.

What eight-year-old needs to weep in broken true repentance? What did they do? Most were just victims of circumstance. And yet they did. The Holy Spirit is Holy! And these children weren't trying to hide their sin nature; they simply allowed His light to expose it, and they would repent and be filled with God. Baptism in the Holy Ghost, even for young ones, was common. God was meeting these broken ones and pouring in such a level of supernatural healing in such a consistent way; it was an amazing thing to see. It was, as the Bakers in Mozambique said, "the cup of blessing and suffering." Broken lives meeting the healing hands of the Potter.

And so we learned. We learned to listen. We learned to watch. It can be a treacherous path for the ignorant. Being full of the Spirit is mandatory, as there is a true ministry of reconciliation given to the church, and then there is the cheaper quality version the world tries to produce. It was around this same time Prime Minister Harper gave out an official apology from the Government of Canada concerning the residential schools. What an evil scheme that was.

Our small understanding began to grow, and we saw how the enemy had attacked the First Nations people with a false Christianity. If I say the name of Jesus while I destroy you, you will learn to hate that name. A very clever tactic by the rulers of the darkness of this world: turn people against their true deliverer by presenting a "Jesus" as an oppressor. And now only the real Jesus can undo the damage with His Spirit moving against that evil imagination. I'll say this as plainly as I can—there is zero true success without the direct ministry of the Holy Ghost.

After Alberta, we moved to the base in B.C., where we would travel with the team doing worship and preaching in remote interior villages. In late November, we were driving up a snowy mountainside on a remote logging road on the way to a village called Takla. Larry said, "Aaron, you're going to preach tonight." And so I did. I wasn't told prior to the trip to prepare any message, but thank the Lord, the Holy Spirit is always ready. I don't remember what I preached on; only that people came forward for prayer afterwards. One lady I prayed for stood out to me, but I didn't really know why. So I prayed, and then soon after, we headed back to base.

When we returned, a lady from our team came over to me and said, "That woman you prayed for at the end, she kept asking, Who is that guy? Who is that guy? Because when you prayed for her, all her grief instantly left, and she had joy. She was laughing."

Now I had remembered her laughing, but people laugh all the time. The Kingdom is righteousness, peace, and joy in the Holy Ghost after all! But what I didn't know is that she had been encased in grief for six years as she had seen her husband and son drown in a canoe right in front of her. But when prayer was given, the Holy Ghost set her free of that horrible bondage. Liberty for the captives indeed! This is why we go.

When you're born again and filled with the Spirit, you have something that can meet the inner needs of people that nothing else can. You have God. God is in that man or that woman. And God wants to work in and through you. Philippians 2:13. Then you shine as lights in the world.

So in 2008 we learned what it meant when God said go. The 'go' is not just a 'where'; though it was west initially, the go is also a 'who'. It is *to* someone—a soul that needs more life and light—someone who hasn't ever had any good news, hearing for perhaps the first time that there is another road, another option, another way out of their troubles and into His Royal Way.

After our time in the west, we returned to Ontario. But there was nothing that seemed to ignite my soul like those rugged days on rough mountain roads, heading towards the lost and hurting. There was nothing glamorous about it. This was a different sort of ministry. There was no fanfare. No hype.

Everyone we knew, if they wanted to "go," wanted to go to exotic places: Hawaii, Switzerland, Morocco, friendly Asian nations. Places where you could be one part missionary, one part tourist. And yes, it's true; all these places can be mission fields. There are people there that need Jesus, and they need someone to bring him. But there are so many parts of the field that are being horribly neglected, as they are not as comfortable as other places.

This is also why it's important to be aware of who in your generation is going into places others don't want to go. Who are the fighters of the faith? Who is pressing the fight to the enemy? Who is reaching where others don't care to reach? We have some good evangelists rising up and some strong pastors these days. We certainly need more teachers in a serious way again. But we have very few ministers that walk, as 1 Corinthians 4:9–13 demonstrates.

In 2008/09, I was able to connect with Rolland Baker, the director of Iris Ministries. (Their personal story of when they went into Mozambique at the end of the civil war should be required reading at any mission school.) We were emailing back and forth for a while, and he was interested in what we were doing with the First Nations, so I was sending him updates.

And then he told me something that is in my heart and on my fridge (when we have one) to this day. He said, "We are very proud of you for accepting this calling. It is exactly the heart of Jesus, and He will be with you, no matter how hard it gets. He will also give you a great deal of joy in your work."

'Well, that's nice,' one might think. 'So he sent you a few encouraging emails.' Yes, one might think it's simply a nicety if one didn't know that he was dying at the time he was writing to me. Heidi and the kids had actually come to say goodbye to him! Yet, in the very midst of that trial, he was still emailing to encourage me in our little work.

That's someone who is dead to themselves and alive to Jesus. That's someone who has stepped beyond comfort. It was a lesson that I'm still learning from. Can you face death and still be an encouragement to someone else? And Rolland didn't die from that foul attack because our Jesus is alive.

Rolland's grandfather was H.A. Baker, who wrote *Visions Beyond the Veil.* It is the first-hand account of orphaned children in the town of Kotchiu, China, having supernatural encounters with the Kingdom of God. A wonderful book. But one I enjoy more, which is less known, is his *God in Ka Do Land.* In it he tells of the endless movement of the Spirit among the remote tribes of inland China and the stories of the genuine sweat and labour to bring the gospel to these unreached and uncomfortable places.

In Matthew 9:38, Jesus doesn't say to pray that the Father sends out *spiritual tourists* into the fields. No. He says, Pray for labourers. Those that are willing to work, to sweat, and to toil—who won't quit—who won't stop—who will go the distance, regardless of the obstacles—the ones that see the harvest MUST come in.

And as we have seen, one of the greatest tools we have in these days to help with harvest is the mighty Holy Ghost. He is the one who will convict the world of sin. Not us! Is it any wonder that Jesus said that the apostles were to wait until they were endued with power from on high?

It is a good lesson for all: Wait until the Holy Ghost comes upon you. Because you can't harvest the world in your own strength. Your great programs won't do it. They won't be enough. You need the help of Heaven. You need the one who actually made the souls that you're trying to see saved. He alone knows how to reach them. He knows what they need and how to be drawn in. Without him, you can do nothing anyway! *Not by might nor by power, but by my Spirit!* Zechariah 4:6. Have truer words been uttered concerning effectiveness?

Without the living spirit of God working with us, our best laid plans will always come up short and empty, never attaining what they should be; never moving one into the Big Life. But with God—working with him and allowing him to move with and through us—this, and only this, unlocks the unlimited potential in the Christian life, especially in the work of missions. Which is essentially, in these last days, the Christian work of harvest.

It was in the year 2000, at a house meeting, when I was baptised with the Holy Ghost. Shannon would be baptised with the Holy Ghost a few months later as she walked home from a Bible study, not long before our wedding in May of 2001. Sometimes you don't know what you need till you receive it.

Right away we saw wonderful healings as God opened to us a world where we can genuinely help change people's lives. We would pray for people on the street and even chase people down in the grocery store. There were no YouTube street healers at that time. There was no YouTube! We just had the Bible and faith in that word. Was I comfortable with it? Not at all at first. But because we knew we had something they needed, we did it. And the more we did it, the more we saw, and the more we saw, the more we wanted to see. God kept expanding our vision for what was possible.

The path of the Spirit, the walking in the Spirit, cannot be fully accomplished without receiving the promise of the Father. The candlestick of your soul can only be set ablaze by the fire of the Holy Spirit! No strange fire here!

Christian missions are under a mandate from Heaven to be endued with power from on high. We are not going merely with good words; we are going with the power of God. 1 Thessalonians 1:5. We cannot do it in our strength; we must do it in His.

The supernatural weapons of Heaven are vital and should not be left aside as though they are optional, as if the Holy Ghost and His gifts are in a "Break in Case of Emergency" glass case. The world is in an emergency!

It is the last moments of the last days, and you, dear reader, need the Holy Ghost! And not to put too fine a point on it; it's not so much because just *you* need him, but there are people out there that need to be set free, and your natural tools simply aren't up to the task. You need the diamond drill of Heaven to get into some of these amazingly hard hearts. You need the dynamite of God to blast out some of these devils that guard the gates. Yes, preach the word, but do it empowered by the Holy Ghost! And then, once you've been to Heaven's armoury, don't be surprised if God starts using you to take aim at the enemy's strongholds—because he will. *The Lord is a man of war: the Lord is his name.* Exodus 15:3

Chapter Five

Attawapiskat

Attawapiskat is a Cree First Nations community situated in Northern Ontario on James Bay, approx. 2000 km north of Toronto. When I first heard about the suicide crisis there, I saw it in a newspaper. It was April 13, 2016, when I read in the Toronto Star, “Ottawa to hold debate on native suicide crisis.” It was a story about a suicide pact between a group of youth. The youngest being eleven years old.

I didn’t know anything about the community, where it was exactly, what people were there... I just knew that *that* sort of thing shouldn’t be going on. Something like that shouldn’t happen. What eleven-year-old doesn’t want to see tomorrow? What kind of situation was up there? So I bought the paper and showed it to Shannon.

Now, what do you do? I didn’t know what to do other than to pray. *Maybe if I can get in touch with someone up there, I can find out what to pray for*. So I started down that path.

I thought, *There must be some sort of church up there that I can get information from.*

So I used that rare gift and wondrously spiritual tool—Google—and searched the name of the town: *Attawapiskat,* coupled with the word *church.* An article came up. It was written by a girl named Faith. It was a picture essay she did about her community. It was simple. Just pictures of buildings in her village. I looked through the photos, and there it was—a church. There *was* a church there. So then I searched for more on the church. I found another article about a native brother, Ross Maracle, doing some work up there for the youth. So then I thought, *Well, if I could get in touch with him, we might be getting somewhere.* So I searched for him. But I was too late. He had died in a car crash in upstate NY. But I noticed the name of the group that had printed the article and decided I'd reach out to them.

It turns out they were something of a missionary info hub. They received reports from about fifty different missionary groups and would then disseminate the information through blogs and email newsletters, informing the public about what was going on in these various places. They were kind enough to forward me the email of a pastor who was up there. I emailed him. The pastor replied that he was shortly leaving the community for the summer, and so he forwarded me to the man who oversaw the work up there. This was on May 20th.

We emailed back and forth a couple times, and I was quite pleased that I was able to inquire about specific prayer needs and let him know that we had seen many wonderful answers to prayer. By May 31st, he had mused on the idea of us coming up while the one pastor was out of the community, so he asked for a list of people he could contact concerning us.

I connected him with various ministers that knew us, including those out west when we first worked among the First Nations. It was interesting to see that what started as a simple request to pray soon became a door where we might be able to actually go to the community.

Soon enough, he heard what he needed to hear from our ministry references, and so he emailed, saying that he wanted to meet in person. We scheduled June 9th in Toronto. Funny thing was though, I wasn't getting paid till the day after the meeting, and when the 9th rolled around, I didn't have any extra funds for gas to Toronto, dinner, and then the ride back home. So what do you do? You move forward!

The group that had initially printed the article that connected me with the pastor up north was about half way, and they had also wanted to show me their ministry media centre, so I figured I'd just head there on the way to Toronto and let God deal with the details. It's his business anyway.

So I set off and met the mission publication group. I toured their facility and learned more about what they do. The owner took me out for lunch to a little Greek restaurant and then handed me $100 after we were done. He said he just "felt" he needed to. And there was the money for the rest of the trip.

How essential the realm of faith is! It can never be oversold. How often we hesitate as we can't see beyond the first step, but the first step unlocks the next, and so on.

So I drove to Toronto. We met. We had what one might call a "theological" dinner. He asked me many questions. Most of them were probing what sort of spiritual position I have: if I was a oneness Pentecostal or a salvation by works guy, etc. We got along well enough on those points. No and no.

Amazing to think that had that $100 not been provided, I would not have been there for that meeting... and so much in this book would never have happened. At least, not by us. It always pays to be bold in your faith.

So after our meal, he decided to start moving things forward to see if we'd be able to get into the community. There were many groups and individuals that guarded that gate, but he started reaching out and meeting with them. He had a key meeting on June 14th with the Aboriginal Pentecostal Ministries leadership and said he would bring up the idea of us going up with them.

While he was meeting with these various groups, we were also meeting with many people. Although those conversations were usually not about us going but rather about why we shouldn't go!

It's surprising, or not, that when you start heading into the promises of God, where, yes, there may be some giants and some walled cities that need to fall in the process, but inevitably there is always the same spirit that was in those ten evil spies, floating around and getting into the mouths of those that know you.

The weeks leading up to us going had many people saying how we shouldn't go into such a large crisis. Especially taking our children to such a place. But if you base your walk with God on the size of the problem instead of the size of your God, you'll never go very far.

On June 22nd, we received the final note of approval. The Chief, the Pastor, the overseer, the Aboriginal Pentecostal Ministries, and the P.A.O.C. had all given us the okay to allow for our access. No one knew us but God.

This is why I say favour is the currency of Heaven. No mission's group was supporting us. Only one church at that time was even praying for us: *Open Door Christian Fellowship*, in London, Ontario. It was the church that Shannon and I had met at. So support for the trip would come in miraculously, just as we would need it, from the few that were aware of our expedition into this new world.

Now, it was one thing to be granted access to the community, but another to discover how to actually get there! We soon found out that our trip would involve planes, trains, and automobiles. So we packed as quickly as we could. I found someone to watch the house. We drove up to Cochrane. Bought tickets on the Polar Bear Express train to Moosonee. Once there, we caught the Air Creebec flight up to Attawapiskat, and just seven days after access was granted, Shannon and me and our three kids, Alaya at 11, Sonja at 9, and Ethan at 4, were standing in the middle of a northern First Nations fly-in-only community, with no man-made plans anywhere to be seen. It would be God's way, or it was no way!

Chapter Six

First Steps

The crisis started when a young girl of thirteen years took her life. What followed was somewhere around one hundred and twenty suicide attempts. Canada's parliament would debate what to do about this crisis for weeks on end.

It was an impossible situation on many fronts, and all we knew for sure was that Jesus could manage it if we could be small enough in ourselves to be the conduits. God's strength is not made perfect when we are strong, but when we are weak. When we have all natural means at our disposal, we actually limit the supernatural. It is a spiritual war, and we need spiritual strength.

Just prior to our hearing that we had been approved to go in, a spirit over that community came to me in a dream and told me not to come and to not bring my children. I had not been directly and preemptively threatened before. Casting out devils and them boasting about their supposed greatness, sure, but this was different. And seeing as we were a couple thousand kilometres from that community, I found that level of threat even more interesting.

Why would the enemy care, or even know, that we were coming to town? But he does care. But not so much about us, but who we carry! This treasure in earthen vessels: Christ in you. This means that when you go, it's not just you that is going; you bring the King! But our defeated foe still has a time making himself like some puffadder to get you to stop moving forward.

Now I know I've touched on this a little, but it is worth repeating. If you're going to step out in the realm of faith to see people set free or to move into a crisis situation, you can be sure that just as the enemy got into Peter's mouth, he will get into the mouths of those around you. People who haven't cared one bit about your Christian walk all of a sudden feel to warn you. This is an outcropping of "the wisdom of the flesh." I have always found that it has a ring of cowardice to it.

So we drove, trained, and flew, listening only to the Lord and his call of compassion and power. Never listen to the wind and the waves for advice.

The flight from Moosonee north, skimming through the clouds above the vast expanse of northern woods and rivers, was a wonderful and new travel experience. We'd seen much of Canada, but this was clearly quite different. It was rugged and raw. Having had a few hours of flying experience myself at that time, it was a great joy to watch our plane land on a dirt runway. You know you're somewhere interesting when it's just dirt you land on.

As a child, I had a vision of flying over hard-to-reach people and dropping sacks of Bibles to them. And now here we were, flying into a remote and desolate situation where the best plans of man were failing and the only thing that could possibly work was the mighty word of God!

The pastor I would be replacing for a time had already left when we arrived, but his wife met us at the airport. She gave us a brief introduction to the town: a community of two thousand Cree living in one square mile of dirt roads and swampy woods. There was one main store, the Northern Store. A spot to get gas. A second store whose origins are dubious, and then there were many little here-and-there stores, but you didn't know they were stores until you went in the house. They would sell pop and chips and "slush," a favourite beverage of the kids; simply ice and flavouring.

The pastor's wife took us to the church and showed us where we could sleep. There was a storage room that Shannon and the kids would put their sleeping bags down in, while I would end up sleeping on the stage, behind the pulpit. This later became a point of interest to some of the kids we would meet.

Some of the pastor's wife's advice to us was that when the bad kids come around, to just lock the church door and call the police. I thought, *That's not really a WWJD sort of thing*. Wasn't that who we've come to reach?

In the article about Attawapiskat from the mission's publication group, they had mentioned in it that the church had added a "youth wing," so Shannon asked the pastor's wife about how many youth they have coming out to church.

"Just one," she said. It was their niece.

The next day, the pastor's wife was supposed to come and show us where to get water, as you couldn't drink the water in town due to it being poisoned by the leeching from a diamond mine 90 km upriver, but she didn't show up. We found out later that she had left town. At least there were a few other believers who came by later that day to introduce themselves to us.

The first lady we met was the definition of stoic. I said "hello" when I opened the church door. She didn't respond and simply walked past me to the front of the church and had a seat.

I said to Shannon, "Maybe you should try and talk to her now... You're a woman."

"You're the Pastor! You should try!" she replied.

I will admit, for a brief second, I wondered what I'd gotten us into. I couldn't even get a "hello" from the first person we met other than the pastor's wife, who evidently didn't think enough of us to show us where one might get water! But one must "crack on," as they say.

Shannon went to the front to speak with her, or at least attempt to. She got a half-smile and a gentle head-roll towards the window as an answer. Well, a gold star for effort anyway! We would eventually get through, and in fact, she would prove to be a great ally, a wonderfully hungry soul, coming to every service and Bible study, learning how to cast out devils, and a mighty prayer warrior who began to share Jesus boldly in the community as an effective witness. A good lesson in persistence in sowing into people. You will reap if you faint not!

Soon enough, a few more people wandered in, and we had some smiling faces, and that made those first few hours easier. There was a young man in his twenties; he was a local nurse, and there were a couple teachers who were leaving town shortly. They came by to encourage us in that old-fashioned, unencouraging way. We were told what's wrong with many things and why Christian things don't often work there. Within minutes, they had pulled Shannon and me aside to pray for them.

I think many Christians are well meaning and sincere but have been taught such wretched doctrine that the potential for Jesus to move through them is almost at a null point due to all the unbelief present. It ought not be so, as there is so much work to do in these last days and so few willing to do it. (But that's going to change!)

The one nurse who showed up had a bit more grit to him, which was good to see. He also played violin, and he had worked in some of the most hostile communities in South America during his nurse training (lots of bullet hole wound dressing) and had done a few remote African trips with YWAM. He told us one wild story of chasing a thief, who had stolen the pastor's phone, through a crowded market while driving a Jeep...armed with guns. I don't exactly recall if it was that he and the pastor had guns, or the thief, but someone did, and either way, chasing a thief through an African market with guns in the mix seems rather counterintuitive on a YWAM trip.

Later that day, he took us on a walking tour of the community, showed us where to get water, and gave us the general skinny on things from his perspective, being at the hospital. He informed us of the massive drug situation.

There were two hundred known drug dealers in town. They actually had an official list that he had seen. That meant one out of every ten people. That's a lot of drugs moving through a community of two thousand people. It was a "dry" community, but that's a very loose term, as at the end of every weekend you could see new bottles in the ditches, and occasionally, people.

The air in the town felt heavy, like it had been in a war. There were burned-out cars. Burned houses. Graffiti and arson were the troubling expressions of the youth. They had to be chased away from the fuel tanks one night. That would have been quite the scene were they successful. Thankfully not.

And as we walked that first afternoon, the whole atmosphere felt as if it were in some sort of coma. I had never been in a place where the very air felt sad. The enemy always manifests his own nature. That's what Powers do. They push a feeling over a place to affect a mindset. And without understanding that you are seated in Heavenly places in Christ, you could succumb to being under its dark clouds. But thank God, who always gives us the victory! 1 Corinthians 15:57. For even as we were told story after story of tragedy and legitimate concern, I couldn't be shaken from the fact that we were walking in the path of Jesus. In spite of the hopelessness being preached to us from the few Christians we met so far, we knew there was a hope we had brought with us that was equal to the task.

Jesus had an uncanny way of moving towards bad news. When you see his life in the gospels and a bad report would come to him, he always responded in the positive. He moved directly towards and against the thing that people saw as a hopeless or impossible situation to solve.

Report: “My servant is sick.”
Jesus: “I will come and heal him.”
Report: “Lazarus is dead.”
Jesus: “You will see the glory of God.”
Report: “They have no food.”
Jesus: “Give ye them to eat.”

Jesus always moves directly against the problem, challenging it. And no matter how great the evil seems, it cannot resist the life and power of Jesus. It couldn’t then, and it sure can’t now. But isn’t that the nature of light? To shine! And the darkness cannot comprehend it!

So as we followed Jesus and his way of pushing past the situation to the heart of the people, he started connecting us to the youth and adults that we came to reach. We were still generally ignorant concerning the full scope of the situation. We knew a little from our time spent out west, but this was a new frontier. It was bigger than what we knew. We didn't fully understand it. But we understood the plan and nature of God, and we knew that Jesus was with us, and he sure made up for any deficiency we had. Hallelujah!

Chapter Seven

Cracking In

So what was the plan? How do we start cracking into such a place? It was a little community, surrounded by hundreds of miles of untouched wilderness. Just thin northern trees, rocks, bears, wolves, and vast emptiness. Once in a while, a polar bear would wander into town. If it was small, they would relocate it. There were seals that would swim up the river, and we even saw a Beluga whale. There was no pretending we were isolated. We were isolated! So what's the key to start accessing such a place?

Well, after our initial walking tour with the nurse, we knew we needed more than just our regular daily prayer and Bible time, so we dedicated Fridays to all-night prayer. 7pm to 7am. The Holy Ghost was the only one who could effectively crack into that place, and if the evil spirit that was up there was so concerned about us coming that it travelled south to challenge us, we knew the enemy's fortifications were not as strong as many of those we met that first day were telling us.

Note: Never let other people's doubt and unbelief be a barometer of what's possible in a situation.

The next day we took a walk to the store. After you get over the initial shock of how high the food prices are, they become comical. The only cheap thing in the north is usually sugar candy. Everything else is around 3-4 times more than what you might find it for in the south. As we were not being supported by any group, it was just faith all around. Faith to eat. Faith to drink. Faith to sleep. Faith to meet people. Faith faith faith. But that's what Jesus is looking for. Luke 18:8.

It was total dependency. The situation far outpaced our natural ability in every way. We were compressed into such a state I had never been in. An all-encompassing realm of the necessity of faith for not just overall victory but daily sustaining. Daily resistance. Daily vision. We were thrown over onto God. There was no *Plan B* in case God didn't come through. There was only *Plan A*—trust in God. Trust His word. Be filled with the Spirit. And from there, as Paul said, "We had the sentence of death in ourselves, that we should not trust in ourselves but in God, which raiseth the dead." 2 Corinthians 1:9.

Faith works when worked.

So after the store, we took our kids to a playground down by the river. It was a playground in name only, for everything was falling apart, graffiti'd, and burned. There was even a suicide note written out on one of the slides. But there were kids there that saw our kids, and as quickly as we arrived, our girls were being greeted and questioned by a small group of native girls. Who are you? Where are you from? Which then became, Where are you staying? Can we come visit?

And once they learned we were at the church, from that day forward we had kids showing up. There wasn't a day where we wouldn't have between four and twenty-five kids doing things at the church or strolling with us through town. And the groups would cycle through. Some days kids from this part of town. The next day, kids from another part of town.

I don't know how word spread that you could just show up at the church, but it seemed most of the kids knew this, as in just a few days, when we'd walk through town, we'd have little ones yell out from their yard, "I know you!" and they'd run to see us or follow us for a while on their bikes and make plans with us to come by the church to do some art or have a meal.

And that was our great plan. Pray. Go for walks. Keep the church door open. Preach the word. Be available for whatever came our way. I remember our first day there, one of the young women who was working in town (she had been put in charge of all the high-risk for suicide teen girls) came by the church to meet us. She asked if we'd be running a vacation Bible school or what programs we had planned. We responded with "none." We weren't there to run programs. As clearly, they weren't working. We were there to bring a living Jesus and would see what He does rather than a program.

At the time of the suicide crisis debate in Ottawa, we heard on the news how the government was sending crisis workers to town and counsellors to deal with the youth. And it's true, there were a few counsellors that had come to town. But most of them couldn't last more than two weeks before they'd have to be cycled out due to their own trauma of hearing so many stories of trauma. But there was only one girl that was in charge of the high-risk for suicide teen girls, and this was her. She was 22. She would have all the girls over to her house each week. She was essentially doing the work of a big sister. A shoulder. An ear. Someone to listen. But it was a far cry from what the government had said they were doing. It wasn't even her specialty. She was just asked to do it because she was there. Eventually she would bring them to the church, which Shannon will share later.

But that is how we started. Within just a couple days, we had a church full of kids and youth. We would give them Bibles. Pray for them. Feed them. Do art. Be whatever was needed at the time. Mother, brother, sister, friend. All things to all people. It was such a contrast to what we were told just a couple days prior—that youth didn't come to the church.

Many would refer to Shannon as mom and myself as dad. When I would call our own girls something like "sweetie," they would laugh and think it was strange. Or if Shannon and I held hands when we were walking, they would giggle. They got a real kick out of seeing even small acts of affection. They longed for family and a place, as that has been one of the great fallouts of the residential schools. And then on top of that, with all the drugs moving through the community, the family becomes splintered and hit with much emotional shrapnel. And the youth, especially the young boys/men, without any direction, coalesce into loose gangs to find some sense of belonging in the midst of a hostile environment.

Now it can seem like every situation you come across is on the negative side of things. Well, there were times for us where it was just life as usual and not everyone we met was down and out; but it's still very much like Jesus said, "They that be whole need not a physician." So when you are available for the Lord, it's only natural that he's going to lead you into certain situations that need him. He's going to draw the ones to you that need him, as that is why He sends you: not to have social meetings, but to see those negative situations bow before the One who is the answer!

Those that think they are doing fine and life is grand very rarely come to the preacher for prayer and comfort! I'm yet to get the midnight phone call from someone who just wanted to say hi and tell me everything is going alright. So until then, we throw ourselves into the darkness like Jesus.

Chapter Eight

The Bad Ones?

He wasn't much more than fourteen at the time, but he was the leader of his gang. They would carry screwdrivers and machetes in case they got jumped. One of them had been arrested five times for moving cocaine. Another showed me a huge scar where the leader stabbed him in the stomach with his machete when they got into a disagreement over something. Another was coming out of drug rehab. He was eleven. They all had arms full of cuts, as that was becoming the norm. Cutting has been fashionable for devils since the man of the Gadarenes.

So these boys came around one night because they heard there was a new "English" preacher in town and they wanted to talk to him. It was quite late when they came by the church the first time, but I came out onto the porch to talk and answered their questions about who we were and why we were there. They informed me that I was English and they were the Canadians.

I let them know that my background was also Polish. "Polish?" they'd ask. "What's that?" And I'd tell them. They seemed to like the idea that I wasn't just English, as these kids viewed the English as the invader. They would yell to me, "Hey Polish!" if they saw me on the road. It made some sort of impression that my background wasn't just English or British. So they decided amongst themselves that I wasn't such a threat to them and so proceeded to tell me more about their personal situations—how the older guys use the young guys to move drugs as they spend little to no time in jail. So after that first night, they'd go walking regularly around town with the not-fully-English pastor.

"You know 4:20?" they asked, and then talked about getting high at seven and eight years old, introduced to it by an older sibling. Only one of them I met had a dad that was at home. And almost all of them wanted a way off the rez but didn't know how. After that initial meeting, they would always come around, dropping into the church to say hi, have a meal, or just hang out and do some art with the other kids.

With their childhood being stolen in order to be tough, they missed out on doing a lot of childlike things. It was quite something to see these young gang kids talking about fighting and drugs one minute, then sitting down with Shannon doing sand art.

Shannon showed a couple of them that their names were in the Bible. "I'm famous!" one would say when he saw it. A boy that Shannon had given a Bible to would ask her where to read from and where the New Testament started. She would show him, and if he forgot, he would quickly ask again. He was genuinely wanting to know how to move down a good road. And then sometimes, the rowdy boys just have to be rowdy.

One Sunday night, they all came to church. Like a pack of stray wolves. The place had gotten quite full, and most of the older folks that knew of these boys were very surprised to see them there.

"These are the worst ones!" Anna said, amazed that they were at the church.

After the service, the old guard filed out, but the group of lads hung around. It seemed they had decided that now, the place being vacant, it might be a good time to fight a little bit. So two of them started rolling into each other, knocking into chairs. The one boy was snarling and growling. It started as a somewhat playfight, but in a moment it was full swings and elbow drops. Once that started, I jumped into the mix to break it up.

Shannon and I corralled them and moved them out of the sanctuary to cool down outside. That took a minute. Shannon noticed a little blood on my neck from the wrangling. It was mine. She informed them that it was late and our kids had to go to bed. The fact that Shannon had kids seemed to come as a shock to one of the boys. "I want to have kids with you," he said to her. You don't hear too many fourteen-year-olds say that to your wife every day.

In the midst of the fighting, it was encouraging to see that the gang leader would eventually join with Shannon and me to deescalate the situation. We could tell he was starting to understand that we were on their side, and in his way, he showed us that he would be on our side as well.

After a few minutes, with the boys being outside and as Shannon and I were chatting inside, we noticed a distinct orange glow coming from the vestibule area. They decided to light some things on fire. Ah yes, boys will be boys! So we informed them that potentially burning down the church isn't the best way to express one's creativity. (This group would try to set the community's fuel storage tanks on fire a few weeks later.) After a stern word from Shannon regarding the nature of the situation, she said quite pointedly, "Don't you realise that you're going to be leaders in the community one day?!" To which one of the boys replied, "Only white people are leaders." Quite the shocking statement. But these boys were used to seeing white people live separately. Most stayed in a little enclave near the hospital. They were the nicest houses in town. But God wanted the kids to relate to us differently. When they saw that we slept on the floor, one of the boys seemed to get a kick out of that and said, "You're sleeping like poor people?!" They actually saw us as lower than them. You know what you can do though when you're lower than someone? You can lift them up.

Shannon continued, "But don't you want to do something with your lives one day?" she pressed.

"I'll just go to Timmins," one said back, and then they spotted some kid on a bike and yelled at him as he was riding past. And then some young woman yelled back at them, after which one of the kids pulled out his screwdriver and said to me, “I might need this,” and charged out into the night, swearing at the girl who was now cussing them out and accusing them of stealing her brother’s bike.

“I’m open! I’m open!” the one boy yelled, challenging a tall teenager who had just showed up with the girl.

I went out onto the porch. The leader looked at me as I watched the situation, and then he gathered his boys up and moved them down the road, with some of them still yelling back at the girl as they disappeared into the northern night, the green of the aurora starting to dance above them.

The leader would be back many times. I would teach him some guitar. We’d go for walks around town where he’d talk about life. Sometimes he’d speed by on his 4-wheeler and take one of us for a ride. We became friends during our initial time there.

One day he brought his little brother over. He wasn’t able to talk and just made sounds. Well, he and Ethan were playing in the church, and then he just started talking. His tongue was loosed, and he became normal. Prior to that, he had a computer that was trying to teach him to speak. But the Holy Ghost has no problem teaching kids how to speak. It just happened. A miracle. A manifestation of the Spirit. An essential reality necessary to change lives, not just "touch" them. The Spirit was always on hand to demonstrate His work for us in so many ways.

The bugs in the north, if you know the north at all, are horrible. There's no other word for it. If it's not a windy day, it's a day spent swatting bugs and smacking the back of your neck. But I did notice that every time this little gang would come by to talk and we'd be on the porch chatting for hours, the bugs would never touch me. It's like the Holy Spirit had a bug forcefield in operation, and as long as I was sharing with these young men, I was untouchable. It was fantastic. I had found the answer for a bug-free life in the north. Just bring a small youth gang with you everywhere and preach the gospel to them as you go.

The first night I was on the church porch sharing Jesus with this gang, I had that memory of eight years prior, when I had bought *The Cross and the Switchblade* with our last seven dollars, and how David Wilkerson was thrust into his new path, starting with youth gangs.

There's one thing about preaching to a group of agitated young men that does something to the gospel. As they were not impressed by my many words nor had the focus for them, I found myself getting to the point much more efficiently than I would when down south. In the south, we've developed a habit of talking about what we're talking about. In the north, you just gotta say it. Say it straight. Say it clear. Say it strong. It completely changed how I teach and preach.

We often miss the strength of preaching by saying words that are just filler, when what people need is the pure, straight arrow of Heaven. The true sword of the Spirit. The unadulterated anointing of the Holy Ghost brought to bear on the problem. People don't need our petty ideas and man-made doctrines that clog the whole machine up. They need God! Did I say that strongly enough? They need GOD!

Many of these young men would come to the church by themselves at various times to talk about their lives. Once they found a safe place with people they could trust, their heart was open. Our big secret was just being available. When there was a knock on the door, be available. When the phone rings, be available. Then let God deal with the details.

Chapter Nine

The Flow

Within a few days of our arrival, it seemed as if the ministry flow God wanted us in was running and running strong. We had a constant cycle of youth coming by. Sometimes, there would be a knock at the door. There'd be a couple kids standing there, and as soon as the door was opened, the person that dropped them off would speed off in their pickup truck, which, I should mention, other than ATV's, is really the only type of vehicle you should drive in such a place, as the roads were a series of potholes with short bridges of dirt between them.

You could get vehicles into town if you put them on the barge that came up, whenever it decided to come up, or you could drive them up on the winter road, which is open for a few weeks deep into winter. It can be a harrowing drive through genuine wilderness and over frozen rivers. It's just you and the wild for hundreds of kilometres.

I heard many stories of people going through the ice or getting stuck in frozen woods with the wolves on the road. The one gang leader I met went through the ice with his dad and their friend who was driving the truck. He and his dad barely got out, but the friend stayed, as he was trying to save his truck, and sat there hammering on the gas. But he wouldn't make it. The truck took him down under the ice, never to be seen again.

Early on we had met a lady, Marilyn, who would be instrumental in opening doors and getting us into the hospital to pray for the sick, but at the time when we met her, she didn't know who the Holy Spirit was or even what a Pentecostal was, not that we were technically "Pentecostals," as I've tried not to attach any title man makes up. We just believe the Bible, from cover to cover, including the cover. But it is a word that at least lets people know you expect the Spirit to move and want to work with him rather than against him.

So Marilyn came by one day and wanted some advice as she was having some issues with the Catholic board in town. She had been attempting to get a lawnmower to cut the grass in the cemetery, but the

Catholic board was, for some reason, blocking her from getting access to the mower.

If anything shows the stultifying choking out of life that a dead religious board can bring, surely blocking lawnmower access for a cemetery does just that. Well, I didn't know much about boards and lawnmower access, but I did tell her, "I think God has better plans for you," and left it at that. She would come back for our first service.

But perhaps one of the most important lessons one needs to learn about the north is their relationship to time. When Einstein said that time is relative, he presented us with a very accurate statement. Allow me to illustrate this with our first Sunday in Attawapiskat: It was 10:30 am. The time we were told by the pastor's wife that church started. Shannon had put the coffee on, as that is an essential part of northern Sunday mornings. (There is no coffee grown in the north, but it is drunk like it is.) Some of the people we had met had mentioned that they played instruments and could help on Sunday with the worship.

I had everything ready to go. I set my Bible on the pulpit, got my message notes out, and waited. And then we waited. And then... waited some more. It was around 11:15 when the first person showed up. And it wasn't even the white teachers. They were even later! But eventually, sometime around 11:30, we had a church with a few folks in it, and some songs started.

It had been a while since I'd been in any remote native community, and I didn't recall the time delay in Alberta and B.C. being such a thing. But I soon learned to just remove my watch. There was no hurry to do anything. Besides, it was more of an event-based time frame anyway. Something would happen on such a day, and it happens when it happens and not before. And when does it happen? When it happens, of course!

Alex, the nurse, had let me know that there was a feast the day before Sunday, as it was Canada Day. He said that the community was having a large meal and gathering down at the river. They had set up a giant Migwam. (What we have often referred to as a Tee-Pee before learning the word Migwam from the Attawapiskat Cree.) But this one by the river was long. It was almost like the Iroquoian longhouses, but it was still angled like a Migwam. The floor was covered with cedar branches, which gave off a wonderful smell when you entered, and there were three large cooking fires, evenly spaced, with giant pots hanging over the middle of the fires. The community elders sat inside along the one wall.

"When will it start?" I asked Alex.

"When you see people going down to the river."

And it was true. It's like when you see a flock of geese on a pond suddenly rise together into the air. What is guiding them? Which one of them said, "Now it's time to fly!" But they all move as one, guided by an invisible God-given sense of timing and purpose. And so it was. I looked out the church window, and people just started heading down to the river, and so I headed down to the river.

Shannon and the kids would stay with the group of girls we had met and make them food at the church. They had been to such a feast many times and so instead wanted to stay with their new southern friends in a new place. I met up with Alex down at the river. That was the first time I ate moosenose. It's as exciting as it sounds, but is a Cree delicacy in that area.

So the whole event was a wonderful lesson on northern time, what it is, and what it isn't. So then I thought, *Feasts may happen when they happen, but surely church still starts on time, as it's church.* But no. No, it doesn't. But at least a service had eventually started. And I preached and taught as I had done in the south. And it seemed to land well enough with the teachers and nurses and some others that were in the community working, but for those from the community, it felt like the message was a bird that just stayed on the wind and never set down.

Now, I must admit that I was not yet used to the stoic faces. I realised later that though you might not see any visible reaction while preaching, yet afterwards they'd tell you how much they liked what you taught. But in the moment, you would think you were sharing a reading from your great-aunt's diary with all the enthusiasm you saw. So I did some adjusting. Some learning. Some growing.

I had to learn how to preach in the north. It was very similar to how I would talk with the gang kids. You don't talk on your way to points. You just get to the point. You preach the point. Every sentence is a complete idea that someone can run with. There's no filler. No, in-between talk. Hit it, and then let the Spirit work!

How we love our many words in the South. Yet we weren't there to just talk. We were there to bring the power and might of the Kingdom of God to bear on an impossible situation. And the talking we did, we made sure it was full of faith.

That was something I noticed right away. The people who were from the south had gotten dangerously casual in their walk. Their mouths bewrayed them. That's how you become a casualty in war—by being casual. Loose lips do indeed sink ships.

Within a few days of our being there, we would be given access to the hospital to play worship songs for elders and pray for the sick. This would happen through Marilyn; she was the lady who initially had come by wanting advice about the Catholic board blocking her lawnmower plans and then had shown up at that first Sunday morning and, through the grace of God, showed up again for our Sunday night.

The worship time that Sunday evening was wonderful. God's presence blessed the people as Alex played the violin, and I strummed along on the guitar. But in the middle of worship, Marilyn got up from her seat and headed to the back. She was overcome by the presence of God and was weeping and didn't want anyone to notice.

She went to the bathroom and then came out to find Shannon, who was standing near the back of the sanctuary, and so asked her, “Why does it make you cry?”

“Oh, yes, isn’t it wonderful!” Shannon replied, but then the Spirit quickened to her that this was a new experience for Marilyn. She had never felt the Spirit of God like this before. She didn’t go to a church like this, if she ever went. Shannon explained to her how this can happen sometimes when the Spirit touches people.

“So it’s ok?” Marilyn asked.

“Yes, it’s a good thing!” Shannon replied.

And this so impressed Marilyn that one could access God in such a way that she started to work for us without us knowing. She started to tell people about us and would bring people by the church for us to pray for. We didn’t need to witness of ourselves; God himself let people know we were there on His behalf. He was our resume.

Now, you may ask, did the Holy Spirit really touch this woman? What evidence might there be in the pragmatic realm? A good question, brother Doubt!

Well, let me tell you about this lady. She was a non-churched, Ph.D. author, native rights activist, and anti-white colonialist. After meeting the Holy Spirit in our service, she offered us her father's old house, as well as land between her sister and brother's places. You know many First Nations activists offering white people their land? I'd say that's evidence of an effect.

That following week, she arranged for me to get into the hospital. They brought some of the elders to a room where her husband and I played for them. We played some tunes in English, and we sang a couple gospel songs in Cree. Those were joyfully received, as most warm to you when you connect in their heart language. After these first few songs, I was allowed to go into different rooms and play music for them and pray for their healing. Within hours of being there, we heard stories from the nurses of people getting better and being filled with joy. People's entire personalities noticeably changed for the better. This is the work of the Spirit. Setting the captives free.

If you are given to God and prayer and become known for prayer, wonderful doors can open for you from the Lord. Another time at the hospital came in such a surprising way that I must recount it so that you can see how essential you are to the Lord and how his desire is to move his life through you to help the world come out of darkness and pain. In desperate situations in the north, it is often that God is the only hope. But what a hope He is! One that doesn't fail!

We were out for a late afternoon walk with a couple kids when a pickup truck slammed on its brakes just as it was passing us. The woman on the passenger side yelled out to me, "Aaron!" I came over to the truck and said hello. The driver was Anna, the one who was overseeing all the high-risk for suicide teen girls. In the back of the truck were the other woman's children. One of whom was the gang leader I had met. They all had hospital masks on and had been crying.

She didn't ask me if I would get in the truck; she told me, "Get in the truck!" So in I jumped and off we sped, leaving Shannon and the kids to continue on their walk. She told Anna to drive her back to the hospital. Anna seemed a little confused as to why, as they had just come from there, but she obediently turned the truck around and headed back to the hospital. As we were en route, I was told that it was her husband who was in the hospital. I didn't know exactly what she wanted from me at that time, but she seemed quite sure she knew. She had never come to any of our church services. But she did know that her little boy could talk after coming to the church.

When we arrived at the hospital, I climbed out, and she told me to follow her. So I did. We went in the main entrance, and she marched right past the reception desk and threw the doors open to the emergency room. The person at reception tried to get my attention, but I wasn't leaving this lady, as she was in such a state it wouldn't have gone well for me. When we arrived in the emergency room, I saw her husband. He was hooked up to a bunch of machines and was on a larger than normal hospital bed. They were prepping him to be flown out. His heart was failing.

To say he was surprised to see me would be an understatement, as he had no shirt on and had those multiple tubes and wires connected to his chest. But his wife didn't care. She was getting what she wanted.

There is a verse in Hebrews 11:35 that says women received their dead raised to life again... and how true it is.

There is something that gets into a woman that they won't be denied, and it can be the most terrifying thing to be around, as a man. It is no wonder Elisha didn't say anything contrary when the woman who lost her son attempted to make her way past Gehazi to Elisha. What were his words to Gehazi? "Let her alone, for her soul is vexed within her." Truly a statement of safety above all else!

And so she declared her purpose to her husband as he nervously looked at me from on the hospital bed. "Aaron is here to pray for you!" she told him. And by this she meant, "Aaron is here to solve this problem." Thankfully, I had the problem solver with me. Hallelujah!

The tone in her voice wanted nothing less than victory. Here lay one of the fathers in town. He was one of the few who still maintained a traditional trapline. He was trying to be there for his children as best he could. His son, the gang leader, would confess to me that he didn't want to be in the gang but had to in order to stay safe and have a position in the community. But what he really wanted to do was go trapping and hunting with his dad. And now here was this devil, trying to destroy this father and ruin that family by taking him away.

How horrible it is when a pastor is called to the side of a dying one, and they pray some half-hearted wondering prayer, as if it may be God's will to take this one home! To remove a father from a family. A loving husband from a wife, or even a young child from a mother. What a doctrine of devils!

And so I prayed for this father and husband. Not the prayer of doubt and wondering, but the prayer of faith. A prayer that is based on "By whose stripes ye were healed." "Believers shall lay hands on the sick, and they shall recover." "Whosoever shall say unto this mountain..." and "The effectual fervent prayer... avails much." 1 Peter 2:24, Mark 16:18, Mark 11:23, and James 5:16.

So my prayer was brief, to the point, and you can be sure that it had heat! I commanded his heart to be healed in the name of Jesus! Laid hands and spoke life to his body. And then I said, Have a good year hunting, and I left. The mother followed me outside, thanked me, and then she and her kids drove off in the pickup truck just as Shannon and our kids arrived at the hospital, and we continued on our walk around town. Just your average evening in the north.

The next day we saw him in his yard skinning some marten, still wearing his hospital bracelet. He had been miraculously healed as soon as I left and didn't need to be flown out to a southern hospital. I saw him years later, still perfectly well, and his son, who was in the gang, had left it and was learning to trap and hunt with his father.

Do you see why it's so important for the body of Christ to walk in the steps of Jesus and not the ignorant confines of dead religion? If we were under some delusion that maybe God was trying to teach him something, or there was some reason he couldn't be healed, then a wife would have lost her husband, the children, their father, the gang leader, a man to follow and look up to. But God knows better.

The word is clear. If Jesus Christ bore it, as Matthew 8:17 declares, then this man doesn't have to. It is the work of the devil trying to attack the word of God. He has no new tricks. But my Bible says, The Lord shall raise him up! James 5:14-15. And so the Lord raised this man up!

That man's healing opened the door to that family's heart. In the years that followed, they'd always call us over to see them, or to have a quick chat, to show us something they're working on, or to hold the new baby. The power is a connector, not just for show.

We carry something wonderful. We carry the potential for a horrible situation to miraculously turn around. The smiles you see on the other side of such a situation are worth every effort you put in to get to such a place, to be available for just such a thing. It is *work* He calls us to; there's no doubt about that, but it's the best work on earth!

Chapter Ten

Brownie Sundaes and Bibles

When Aaron asked me to share a couple testimonies from our times up north, my first thought was, "There are so many; how do I choose?" Indeed, my journal is full of experiences: the good, the bad, the ugly, the sublime. A week in Attawapiskat feels like a month, and a month feels like a year as far as experiences go. But without even having to reference my journal, there are those certain gems that stand out, and I can recall them as if they happened yesterday. This is one of them.

My journal records this as happening near the end of our first stay in Attawapiskat, Aug. 6, 2016. Anna, the young social worker in charge of the high-risk for suicide girls in the 12-16 age group, asked me if it would be okay to have a "girls' night" at the church. She needed a space that would be safe and private for her girls, and Anna (being a Christian also), felt that the church would be the right place for them to have a little party. Normally they'd get together at Anna's small residence or go into the bush for a campfire. Sometimes we'd see them bomb around the community on four-wheelers or going for walks together in a big group. The girls would shout at us and say "Hey Blondies!" as all three of my children stood out with their blond hair.

Being not much older than these girls, at 22, Anna could be a friend as well as a counsellor and seemed to be doing a good job keeping the girls accountable and spending that all-important quality time with them. A little love goes a long way in the hard north.

So of course I agreed to host, and Anna planned a fun night of pizza and brownie sundaes, with card games, nail painting, and bracelet making. Aaron took our kids to Anna's place, as advised by Anna, who couldn't promise G-rated language from her girls.

Before they came, I walked the floor of the church, praying over the night. Specifically, that God would make His presence known in some way and touch the hearts of the girls. Knowing that the night wasn't going to be a "church event" (other than to provide the space) and that most of these girls, if not all, weren't Christians, I prayed that God would give me an opportunity in the midst of the "party" to minister to someone. As I was walking and praying this out, I literally hit an invisible spiritual wall. It was hard and it hurt, and I thought, "This is going to be an interesting night."

Now, up until this time, we had mostly dealt with the kids–lots of them–and adults. We had some dealing with the "bad boys," as Aaron has mentioned, and I had met a couple of the teenage girls when we first arrived. But on the whole, this particular age group and the nature of it (high risk: meaning they had either attempted suicide or showed signs of it) we had little contact with. So when they showed up, I was certainly aware of the atmosphere shift.

A group of teenage girls piled into the church, many in oversized hoodies and sweatpants. Some of them looked like boys, and I almost told them that it was girls only (thank God I didn't!) I'll admit, they looked tough but hurt. The mom in me wanted so much to sit down with them one on one and tell each of them about God's love, but I knew that wouldn't be possible in this context, so I just left it up to whatever God was going to do. Anna put some music on (the likes of which I'm certain had never graced the interior of the church before), and our girls night was under way.

Frozen pizzas were soon bubbling in the oven. The girls were now loud and apparently having a good time, and I was busy cutting a tray of brownies for our sundaes when I felt someone beside me. I turned to see a very mean-looking girl towering over me in size, just standing there as close to me as she could get, with a look that meant to intimidate me. I said something nice and polite while I continued to cut the brownies. No response.

She stepped even closer and put her face right in mine. I looked at her again and met her with the same stare she was giving me. I felt like I was staring down a bull who was about to charge. What was she doing?

I was aware of how big the knife I was using was and hoped that she wasn't going to try and grab it. We just stood there looking at each other like this. Then something broke the stare.

I suddenly found myself laughing at the situation! My laughter softened whatever it was in her that was trying to threaten me, and she laughed it off too, slapping my shoulder and saying "Nah" as she walked away.

After that, I heaped ice cream on top of the brownies and drowned them in chocolate sauce, and then quickly got out of the way as the group of girls rushed the table of sweets!

As the night progressed, I was starting to feel discouraged. The music was so loud that it was hard to talk. The card games were becoming more rowdy, with girls pushing each other off their chairs in playful chaos whilst a tumbleweed rolled past the empty corner where the nail polishing table was. (Apparently not a hit with these girls!)

I parked myself at the bracelet-making table and waited for the arrival of 9:00 and the end of our girl's night. I found it difficult to connect with any of the girls. They were either really loud and throwing cards or silent and introverted. I've never encountered this level of introversion like I have in the First Nation communities. I've literally seen girls with the drawstrings of their hoodies pulled so tight around their faces that you can barely see them. Likewise, I've asked some girls what their names are and have had them respond by shaking their heads 'no'. That kind of fear and shame is a heartbreaking reality for so many teenagers today.

Around the completion of my fifth bracelet, a woman showed up with her three little girls. I don't know why she was there, but she just came in and sat down beside me, and we started to chat. It was nice to finally be able to engage in conversation with someone. I showed her and her kids how to make a bracelet. She showed me the scars on her arms from cutting when she was "their age," she said, pointing to the teenagers. She told me how she used to suffer so badly from depression.

I looked at her young daughters and thought about how innocent they are now—and how common it is to see innocence turn into depressed, cutting teenagers. After a night of being around these high-risk girls, it was refreshing to see the sweet young faces of her little ones. The four-year-old smiled at me and then gave her mom the finger! Innocence has a short run in Attawapiskat.

As we sat together making bracelets, I was able to talk to this woman about the Lord and how He can set us free. She said that her nine-year-old used to go to Sunday school, but then she lost her Bible and doesn't go anymore.

I turned to the 9-year-old and said, "Do you want another Bible? I can give you one right now!" She nodded, and I jumped up and went to the storage room, where there were boxes of Bibles donated to the church. Since our arrival in Attawapiskat, we had been working our way through these boxes, giving Bibles to whoever wanted one.

I brought out a box and set it on the same table where the brownie sundaes used to be. I gave the 9-year-old a Bible, and one of the girls playing cards said, "Hey, what's that?"

"A Bible," I replied.

"Can I have one?" she asked.

"Of course you can," I said, and then handed her one.

And then one of the greatest things I have ever seen took place: those high-risk for suicide teenage girls rushed towards that box of Bibles with more frenzied excitement than they did over the brownie sundaes! I stood back and watched as they all grabbed a Bible, saying, “I want one!” "Save one for me!” I took notice of a girl that didn’t want a brownie sundae—but she took a Bible! It was glorious.

Anna just looked at me with wide eyes. She was amazed! And there it was: the answer to my prayer. I may not have been able to connect with those girls that night, but Jesus sure did! He is the Word—and they wanted that. They wanted him. Praise God.

At 9:00, with Bibles in hand, these girls filed out of the church, thumping my shoulder and smiling at me on the way out. Anna stood there with me on the church steps and said, “I’m shocked! I’ve been working with these girls for a while now, and some of them are so hardened towards God. I can’t believe they all wanted a Bible!”

Aaron and the kids came back to the church as the girls were leaving, and I was so excited to tell them what happened! Never underestimate the pace at which the Lord moves and the ways in which he chooses to answer prayer.

And in the morning, there were no Bibles in the ditches!

Chapter Eleven

Kingdom Days

Every day was filled with God. When we first arrived, the town felt distant, heavy, and foreboding. But now, the air was electric, buzzing with an unlimited potential for the miraculous. It was the Christianity of my childhood, finally being lived out again. Where Jesus and his Kingdom are offered without any excuses, amendments, or provisos.

We would see extraordinary things. Things you read about in the Bible. And then they'd happen so effortlessly. And in most cases, without you realising what was actually going on until after.

There was never a "who wants to see a miracle?" announcement. You just did what was right according to the word, and if a miracle was needed, it would happen.

One day, while we were feeding kids, as was so often the way, Shannon was making grilled cheese. We had a bit of bread and cheese left from the morning, and there were a couple kids with us that day, so there it was: A simple problem of lunch was solved. But then more kids came in, and more kids came in, and everyone was hungry. So Shannon just kept making grilled cheese. And then more kids would arrive, and Shannon would make more grilled cheese. And it wasn't until after all the kids had eaten and asked for no more that she realised what had just happened.

We didn't have enough bread or cheese for all those kids that showed up. So the Jesus that multiplied bread and fish multiplied bread and cheese.

But you can be sure if Shannon had started to get nervous about all the children coming in; this story wouldn't be here, but she didn't. She just operated in love, which she does so well, and her faith, which works by love, was on hand so Jesus could feed the little children!

One of the first prophecies Shannon ever received was about being a mother of Israel with a wide lap that would receive children, both young and old. That has been so true as I've watched her minister over these many years. She becomes "mom" to many a little and big person!

On another occasion, we had met a lady who was hungry for the things of the Spirit of God, and so we wanted to have her and her kids over for dinner. She was coming back to the Lord after practicing native spirituality. She discovered it didn't bring the peace she was hoping for, so she wanted Jesus. She wanted the real Jesus.

She was living with four kids in a shack with no finished interior walls (they were just framed), no exterior insulation, and no running water. All their clothes were in garbage bags. It could take a long time to get a house, and much of that depended on your relationship with those in the band office. (A lady we know waited almost 30 years to get a house.)

So naturally, with such a hard living situation, we wanted to bless this woman and her kids with a larger than normal meal. You know, really bless 'em.

That day I was playing music for the elders at the cemetery. They had successfully navigated the gauntlet of the Catholic board and had cut the lawn somehow and were celebrating their success with a few sandwiches and lemonade, and they wanted me to play them some gospel songs while they sat and listened. That was certainly a new spot to play.

So I had gone off to do just that, which ended up being rather interesting as a medicine man showed up and stuck his staff into a grave and was drooling over it. But that's a story for another time.

Shannon and the kids were making their way to us when Shannon came across a stack of twenty-dollar bills on the road. She hadn't seen them until she was just stepping over them. And there they were. All neatly stacked in the middle of the dusty road. Just what we needed to cover the cost of the dinner that night.

There was a man a few hundred feet ahead of Shannon, and so naturally, as one does, she thought, maybe he dropped this money. So she caught up to him, showed him the money, and asked if he dropped it. Well, Shannon spoke a little more Cree than he spoke English, but he made it clear that it wasn't his. So there it was. The provision for the meal. And this sort of miracle would happen twice in the dust and many times in our account. Funds showing up just when we needed them.

Now, I had seen the same sort of thing as a boy: God providing money supernaturally. Shannon and I had also seen it throughout our marriage: God working his work to provide what was required.

One time we needed just fifty cents to run a dryer, and so we prayed, and then after our prayer there were two quarters for the dryer on our kitchen counter that hadn't been there.

Another time we didn't have a phone line, but we needed to make a call to see about getting a certain apartment. We had an old phone, but the line was not on, and neither of us had a cellphone at that time.

So we prayed that God would somehow give us a phone line. We said, "Amen," and then when we picked up the phone after the prayer, there was an active phone line.

For those of you who don't know, a phone line used to be for telephones that people would have in their houses. It was a wire. The phones attached to these lines would stay there at the house as they didn't fit in a backpocket so well. These phones would sometimes be on a wall or sometimes on a table. You could not talk to the phone; they were not smart.

The active line lasted until the day we signed the lease on the new place. That very same day, the phone line simply shut off. Job done.

Even recently, when we were leaving New Brunswick to head back to Ontario, we needed exactly $1000. We didn't have it that morning when we were told we needed it. But shortly after this, I checked my account. Someone had just deposited $1,000. There was no e-transfer name/email. It was a direct account deposit. (No one has our account number.) It couldn't be traced to anyone or any entity. God knows his business.

Another time, when we were driving back from the Yukon, people were praying that we would make it to Stratford. And we did, by a mixture of chicken wire, angel feathers, and the prayers of Ray and Marlene Shantz. The moment we arrived in Stratford, I stopped our vehicle to run into a store. When I went to start it again, it wouldn't go. The engine was dead. The next day it went off to the wreckers. So we got to Stratford, but we had a problem; we needed to get to Wemindji, 2000 km north. We met with the local brothers that knew us and let them know we were on our way to

Wemindji, where I would be pastoring the church. We were due to leave in a week. Our friend, Doug Butler, who has known our family for 40 years, announced at Jubilee Stratford that we were heading up, and if anyone would like to help us with that, they could. Within 16 hours, we purchased a van to make the trip! God knows his business. Many were saved, healed, and delivered because of this partnership, and as such will go on Jubilee's heavenly account as well!

And like I've learned so often, power and miracles happen when we are at a point of weakness. It is there we see His grace and His strength.

When did Jesus turn water into wine? When they had no wine. When did Jesus multiply bread and fish? When they didn't have enough bread and fish. When did Jesus walk on the water? When he didn't have a boat. Why do the lame walk? Because they couldn't. When did the money come from the fish? When there was none in the pocket. So you see, it's the low places that are the breeding ground for miracles. God fills those valleys with his glory, and occasionally, He will fill your guitar!

One day we had been given a friend's canoe, and we were paddling up the river all afternoon. It is quite a nice escape to be out on the river and away from the bugs. But it is a strong northern river in places, so you work most of the time as you cross it.

After one such day, we arrived back at the church around 6:30 pm and were planning a nice evening of laying on the cool church floor and doing very little else when the phone rang.

It was Marilyn, the lady who had gotten me into the hospital to pray for the sick and who had encountered the Holy Spirit that first Sunday night. She asked me if I could bring my guitar down to the river to play some gospel music.

Everything in my flesh was shouting no! Even logically. I was quite exhausted from the afternoon trek, but it didn't matter. When you're in such a place and there is a demand placed on a gift you have, you say yes. You move into the territory. You take the land, no matter how you feel. Always take ground.

So I got my guitar and headed down the dusty road. When I arrived at the river, I noticed they had set up a couple speakers and a little mixer. They were serious about me playing! So I plugged in my guitar.

There was no one there. It was just me and the couple that asked me to come down, and so I started to play.

Now, in the north, there is only one overarching style of Christian music. (At least, in the north I've been.) And that is the old-fashioned country gospel. That's what you sing. They're often simple songs. But they're often scriptural. And they go good with a large cowboy hat.

It reminded me very much of when we lived in Texas. How that style of music got adopted in the north, I'll never know, but it must be simply from how they travel like nobody's business. I don't think anyone on earth travels like these from the north do. They can be up on James Bay one day, down in Arizona a couple days later, and then out in Saskatchewan seeing a cousin and going to some tent revival meeting, and then back for supper without breaking a sweat. And some people won't drive more than 15 minutes to go to church! But if country gospel can travel from the Bible Belt in America to the far north in Canada, well, surely you can walk down to the river to play some of those songs!

So on this day, that's what I was playing. And then people started showing up—wandering down to the river. Trucks were pulling up. People were looking out of their houses. Soon there was a crowd of people on the shore and back, scattered over a few hundred metres. And so I kept playing as the people kept coming. They might yell out a song they'd like to hear, and if I knew it, off I'd go into it. It seemed *Jesus on the Mainline* was so well received, I'm pretty sure I was asked to play it three times. I was tired, but honestly, who cares if you're tired? You're there to serve. That's often all He asks of us. Just be faithful with the little things.

And then it was done. I packed up the guitar, greeted a few folks, and headed back to the church as the sun was setting. Northern cowboy. And like so many times, it's afterwards that you find out what God was up to.

While I was playing, waves of energy were rolling out from the Spirit of God from where I was standing and knocking into the crowd. People were being knocked around. Women were weeping out in the open and being delivered. No hands laid on them.

No words spoken. Just praise ascending to God and the power of the Spirit moving through it. Psalm 22:3.

I found all this out as I was walking back to the church, having felt nothing at the time but tired. No "miracle chord" moments for Aaron. But God always extends beyond us. Beyond what we see or feel. He's always able to do more than what we're expecting.

Marilyn, who had asked me to come down, was overjoyed. She was smiling so big and wide and had a look on her face as if to say, "That's why I asked you to come down to the river. So that would happen!" She rode next to me on a bicycle as I walked back to the church, in awe of the things God was doing while I was just tired and strumming and singing.

She said, "People are finding out about the Holy Spirit!" And she was right! Once she realised that the Holy Spirit could engage people in the real world, like she had been that one Sunday night, she made it her mission to make opportunities for him to work through us and very often would bring people by for prayer or take us places to pray for elders or those who couldn't get out.

After that evening at the river, I'd have people in town making song requests as they'd see me walking around. They'd stop next to me in their trucks or yell at me from their porch, "Hey! Next time play...such and such!" Some would call me "The Man in Black," but I don't recall playing any Johnny Cash.

It's fascinating to see how God starts opening a community to you. How he weaves you into the fabric of people's hearts. A man's gift makes room for him indeed. And not just my gift and my hands. All of ours. Every crafty thing Shannon and the girls could do got utilized in some way. If there was something God put in you, it was coming out! Just be available and faithful and watch for God.

Shortly after the evening at the river, I got a call at the church from someone in town. It was the Chief. He wanted to meet. He wanted to talk to me in person.

Now, I don't know if it's because I would get in trouble as a kid at public school for being a little too much of myself, but the Chief and the idea of a school principal seemed very close in my mind, so I was expecting him to come and tell me why he's going to evict us from the community (known as a BCR: Band Council Resolution) or make me write a lot of lines on a blackboard during recess.

He showed up in his pickup truck. When he met me at the church door, he simply said, "Let's go for a drive." And off we went. This was the Chief that met with the Prime Minister in Ottawa and scolded him for not helping enough. So I knew this chief wouldn't pull any punches.

He started down a road I hadn't previously seen, driving a ways towards a large wooden rehab building that was tucked back around the corner of the community. *This would be a good spot to dispose of a white preacher I didn't like*, I thought.

On our drive, he began to tell me about some of the issues he was dealing with in the community. He talked about his recent trip to Ottawa and what he said to the Prime Minister. How he scolded him. He talked about the treaty they were under. What the expectations were.

When you learn about native things in school from your liberal teacher because it's First Nations week is one thing, but when a prominent Chief is telling you how it is for real while he's driving you around in his truck on his reserve, well, that's a whole other perspective.

We drove around for a little over two hours. That was an education. He didn't waste any of his time and wanted to be sure I was fully informed about the region. After his overview of what he's been dealing with, he said, "I've heard what you've been doing here. How you're treating our people. I hear everything you're doing. Everyone tells me..."

I started to sweat like I was in the principal's office. But then he continued, "You are doing a good thing for my people here. You are doing things the right way... I want to bless you."

I was amazed. The Lord truly encompasses us with favour, as with a shield! He had even heard about us sleeping on the floor. What's interesting about that is how Jesus showed Shannon we were to come into the community. Like Jesus did he on Palm Sunday lowly. Come in low. Take the humble path.

Not that you would come in blowing a trumpet; however, there was a group that came up while we were there. They rented an expensive black helicopter and announced themselves on the community webpage as if the cavalry had arrived. They did not end up being welcomed, and in fact would complain to a friend of ours who was assigned to them as a liaison that the people should be glad they were there. The very opposite of how Jesus would do it! Take the low seat. And Jesus can always bring you higher.

The Chief and I would meet again in the south, at Kettle Point First Nation, a couple years after this, and he told me that when my name came across his desk regarding our getting access to the community, he knew he didn't know me, but he felt in himself to let me in. He didn't know why, but he granted the access. Of all the people and groups that opened the door for us, none was more important than the Chief. If everyone else had said yes and he had said no, we never would have been able to go. Favour is the currency of Heaven.

The McGill Family 2016

The Northern Call

First Flight

First Feast

Praise March

Prayer Circle Attawapiskat

On the Rock

Four Friends

More Friends

Exploring

Three Amigos

Aaron & Patrick Downie with Mural

Dusty Days

Cultural Bridge

Universal Language

Hanging Out

4-Wheelin'

Braid and Seek

Puppy Love

Wolf Pack

Rez Truck Before

And After

Water & Ice

Looking at You

Faith Chapel

Where Angels Sang

Grey Hoodie Gang

Cree Stop

Winter Road Moosonee

Wemindji Winter

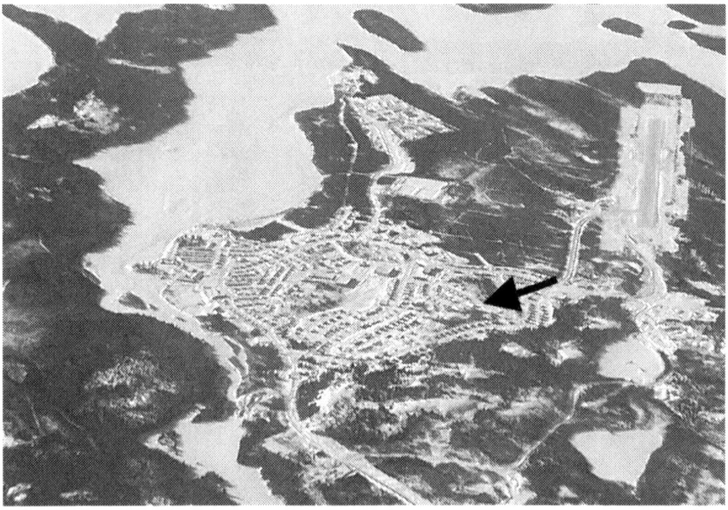

Miracle Van

Deliverance

Wemindji Heights

Shannon's Favourite Part

Northern Exposure

Aurora Borealis

Migwam Walk

Circle of Friends 2023

Baptism

After Baptism

Preaching

Teaching

Migwam Roast

Cookies and Tea

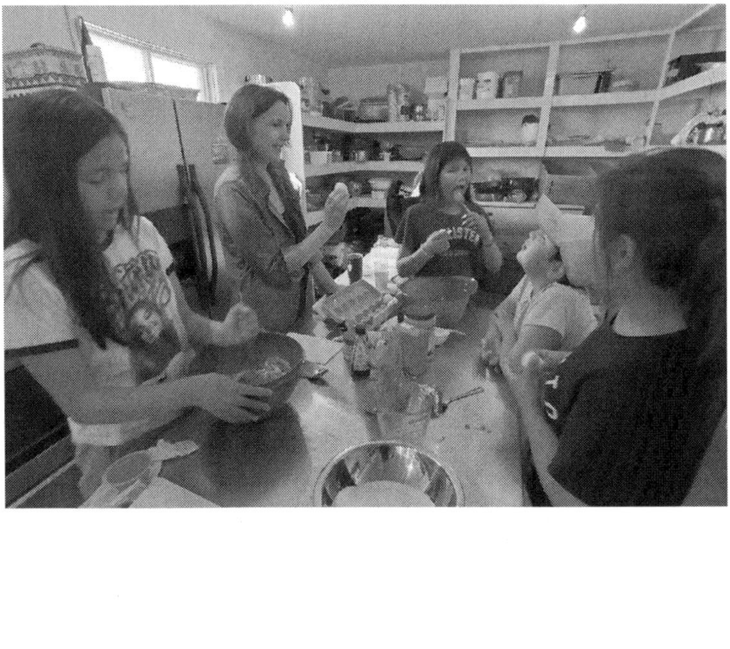

Sisters with Sisters

Prayer Circle Wemindji

Chapter Twelve

I Think I Just Saw Jesus!

When we first arrived in Attawapiskat, it was an eye-opener, to say the least. Aaron has already gone into detail of our first impressions, so I won't add much more to that—except to say that we found ourselves in what appeared to be a forsaken land. The remote isolation combined with severe poverty was shocking, and we had to remind ourselves that we were still in Canada!

But despite the poor housing situation and burnt-out cars and vandalism, kids are still kids, whether they're in a palace or a ghetto.

It was Canada Day, 2016, and we decided to venture out and see if the rumours of a parade were true, and sure enough we found ourselves watching a line of about 50 cars and four-wheelers decked out in Canada flags with everyone honking horns and waving at us. At that moment they weren't First Nations, and we weren't white—we were all just Canadians together.

This procession drove around the small community for the better part of the afternoon.

After that, we went to the "playground"—a sad and broken-down place for kids, with bad words written all over the tilted and melted slide that someone had apparently tried to set on fire. The swingset was missing the swings, the park bench was missing the bench, and there was litter in every place but the garbage can.

As we heavily supervised our four-year-old on this vulnerable apparatus, three young girls shyly approached us. They were about the same ages as our girls, and once we started talking with them, they were anything but shy. Shania, Melissa, and Clara became our fast friends, spending the whole day with us and every day after that.

Attawapiskat is a land of children, and we always had kids with us, but I have to admit, I had a favourite, and it was Shania. She was about nine years old and sharp as a knife. She knew everything about her community and everyone in it. She had a very traditional and stoic face with piercing eyes, but she could also make us laugh till we cried, and she was a rascal.

Our "kids" went everywhere with us, and so we had lots of opportunities to talk with them about God. We soon found out how sensitive to the spiritual realm these kids were. They'd tell us about the spirits they'd see and the voices they'd hear in the wind. One time when the kids were all playing a game in the church, one of the girls, Clara, saw a "spirit girl" standing in the corner. When I asked what she was doing, she said, "Just watching us." Needless to say, Aaron and I had to deal with this spirit and many others.

Syncretism is common in Attawapiskat. The cross and the dreamcatcher are side by side on living room walls. When we ask the kids if they believe in Jesus, they say, "We believe in everything." So how do we really reach these kids with the gospel?

So much of being around children is seed planting. We show them the love of God by simply being there with them—bringing them into our family, going for walks, making cookies, opening the door to their knocks at all hours, telling them that stealing is wrong and how they should return the stolen loot that they proudly show us, inviting them to church, and then trying to keep them quiet once they're there and hoping that some of it sticks. We listen to them and get to know their world. They would tell us about their lives, and we realized that all of them knew someone who had committed suicide.

Naturally, we became attached to many of these kids, despite their often bad behaviour (and sometimes because of it). After pouring so much into Shania's life, I couldn't help but be disappointed when I caught her and a friend breaking into the church to steal chips from the cupboard. Teaching the kids not to steal was difficult because they were just so used to it and didn't ever feel the consequences of it. But when Shania looked at me as she hurried out the backdoor, I knew she felt it. I forgave her immediately, of course, but she didn't know that because the shame and guilt of it kept her away from coming around after that, and a couple days later she flew out of town with a relative and wouldn't be back until after our departure.

I found this out only after she left and felt bad that I didn't get to say goodbye to her and let her know that there were no hard feelings.

Two years later, we came back to Attawapiskat, and I was so happy to see a taller, but still the same Shania! I gave her a hug and pressed my cheek against hers. Once again, she was shy at first, but just like the last time, she warmed up to us, and we were right back to where we left off from two years before. This time, with two years added to her maturity, Shania was all the wiser to the ways of her community.

One afternoon she took me and my kids around town to say 'Hi' to all our old friends. We were out later than expected, and I found myself and my children in the thick of an Attawapiskat night without Aaron, but oddly enough, I felt totally safe with Shania.

She could see someone approaching in the dark and tell me who it was before I could even make out that anyone was there. She had night vision and a keen street sense. Whenever a shady person approached us, she'd cut them with a lash from her tongue, and they'd scurry away.

Every house we passed, Shania would tell me everything about its inhabitants. I thought to myself, "This girl should be Chief!"

Shania got us home safe and sound, and then Aaron walked *her* home—although I'm sure she didn't need his protection!

In the days that followed, we saw a lot of all our kids again, and this time I was even more determined to explain salvation to them. Being a couple years older, they might be more ready to listen and pay more attention now to our words and not just our actions. I prayed specifically to have an opportunity to speak into Shania's life and asked God to prepare her heart to receive him. Of course I wanted this for all the kids—but there was something about Shania that made me single her out for such a time as this.

The sooner these kids meet the Lord, the better. That can be said for all of us, but life in Attawapiskat is hard, and childhood is short, and I was determined to leave this time knowing that I was leaving Shania in good hands!

So one day, when a group of us were going to the big rock (a huge boulder covered in spray paint that the kids would climb up on), Shania pointed to the sky and said, "Did you see that?"

She was pointing to the sky above Potato Island (an island in the Attawapiskat River where the first missionaries planted potatoes years ago).

We all said, "See what?"

She said, "A big white thing with stretched out arms over Potato Island... I think I just saw Jesus!"

Well, that certainly got my attention! She described it again, and the other kids with us said, "Nah, you lie." But there wasn't a trace of deception in her. She was as genuine as I had ever seen her. I knew this was it: the answer to my prayer for Shania—God was preparing her heart to receive him!

When we got to the rock, the kids climbed to the top, and while the native girls were braiding my daughter's blond hair (they endured lots of this), I was taking pictures and thanking the Lord for what he was doing. The sky was a clear blue. There was no rain, but a big rainbow appeared. Shania started talking again about the white figure in the sky, and so I used this opportunity to talk to them about salvation.

Reading over this experience in my journal brings it all back so clearly. I told Shania that God often shows Himself to people in different ways when

He wants to reveal Himself more to them and be in their lives. I let Shania know that God was trying to get her attention because He wanted to be in her life. I told her that the only way we can really know Jesus is by asking him to come into our hearts and receive him as our Saviour.

I was careful not to make anything sound religious; they were used to religion from the Catholic church in town, and I didn't lead them into the sinner's prayer. I simply told Shania that whenever she wants to, she can ask Jesus to come into her heart, and He will change her life and always be with her. She listened and kept her piercing eyes on me. I asked her if she understood. She nodded, then asked for my phone to take pictures. Sometimes it's so hard to know if you're getting through!

So after our time on the rock was done, we went back to the place we were staying, and the kids went next door to jump on the trampoline while I had a very necessary tea. Time to oneself is rare on any mission field, so you take it whenever you can get it.

Just as I was sitting down with my tea and beginning to write this account down in my journal, in walks Shania by herself. “How perfect,” I thought. Now I could get into it a little deeper with her.

I made her a cup of tea, and then we talked more about the Lord. I explained salvation more in depth and told her about sin nature, the cross, our redemption, the devil, our sins being paid for... Keeping it as simple as the gospel actually is. I could tell that I was getting through to her. I told her that the only way to get to Heaven is through Jesus. She didn’t know this before.

I desperately wanted Shania to see how easy salvation is. I wanted her to grow up in Attawapiskat with Jesus. I wanted her to be in Heaven.

Then another girl, Bobby-Jean, came in, and Shania said, “We’re talking about Jesus!” Bobby-Jean said, “I don’t pray.” So we talked about how it’s hard to talk to someone you don’t know and how, in order to know the one you’re praying to, you first have to have him on the inside of you. This is what we have to do with Jesus in order to have a relationship with him.

Bobby Jean said, “How?”

I said, “By asking Jesus to come into your heart and be your saviour.”

Bobby-Jean shouted, "Jesus, come into my heart!" And she and Shania laughed—but I said, "It's as easy as that—and if you really meant it, He's there right now." They looked at each other with wide eyes. I explained how it's not just the words, but the heart also, as Romans 10:9 says, "That if thou shalt confess with thy mouth the Lord Jesus and shalt believe in thine heart that God hath raised him from the dead, thou shalt be saved."

We talked some more, and they told me about some people in their lives who have hurt them. I told them how everyone needs Jesus and how once he's in us, we can pray for those around us to receive him too. I wanted so much to reach these girls. Attawapiskat is a hard place to grow up in—too hard without Jesus.

The girls asked for more tea...and can we make cookies too? Sigh. I want them to want Jesus—not tea and cookies.

It was time to go to church for the evening service, so off we went. Our little group of friends, walking down the dusty road in a brilliant pink Attawapiskat sunset.

I strayed back a bit and took a mental picture that I can see clearly before me now as I write it: My children (including my native ones who called me mom that summer), walking happily to church on a summer evening with that glorious sunset lighting up the dusty street and transforming that poverty-stricken town into streets of gold.

I remember thinking to myself, "This is the life; talking to the kids about the Lord all day, then walking to the rickety old Pentecostal church on a soft summer night on the rez—I could do this for the rest of my life!"

Later that night, when church was done and we were back home, burning more mosquito coil and getting ready for bed, my daughter Alaya came up to me and said, "Mom, tonight when we were walking to church, Shania went off on her own a little, and I heard her say, 'Jesus, come into my heart and be my saviour!' Shania got saved tonight!"

Thank you, Jesus.

Chapter Thirteen

The Valley of the Shadow

There's a great many things that people say cause suicide, but what we see in the word of God is that this is a primary sphere of the devil. It's not just you being depressed. It's spiritual. When death is involved, it's the height of spiritual warfare.

When the devil came to Eve in the garden, he could not destroy them. So he needed them to destroy themselves. He needed them to kill themselves by disobeying God. He did the same thing when he tempted Jesus. He took him to the pinnacle of the temple and told him to throw himself down, and then misquoted Psalm 91 as part of his deception. He couldn't kill Jesus, so he attempted to get him to kill himself.

Now, the Bible doesn't technically say there's a *spirit of suicide*, but we understand the nature of unclean spirits and devils in general in the word. A very clear case is when we see them working in the man of the Gadarenes in Luke 8. For when the devils are cast out and go into the pigs, we see a mass suicide. Suicide can be the ultimate effect of any unclean spirit or devil once it gains dominance over the will of the individual.

Now, the Bible does tell us that the last enemy that will be destroyed is death. See 1 Corinthians 15:26. Death is an enemy, just as the dragon, the beast, and the false prophet are listed as enemies.

But more to the broader point, the whole focus under the devil's kingdom of darkness is death. Death of anything God has made. As we are told, the thief comes to kill, steal, and to destroy. John 10:10. And as man is God's chief creation, a devil, no matter what kind, moves its prisoner towards destruction and death—either through prolonged sickness to weaken the body, or through emotional destruction to weaken the mind and will, or through, what the Bible calls, doctrines of devils, which will lead one from the path of the truth of God into a place of lies, confusion, doubt, and fear. But at the heart of it all is deception.

It is a lie that there is no hope. There is always hope because there is always Jesus. But when children don't have Jesus or a real understanding of being able to unburden yourself (the weights and pressures) on him, or they don't know how to cast devils out, or they don't have a mechanism to cope with the emotional overload, then we will see nothing but a land of destroyed youth.

Now perhaps someone has just thought, Why would you teach a child to cast out devils? A valuable question, even more so when you realise how often children deal with the demonic and how parents are failing in their seriousness to stem this tide.

Even our daughter Alaya had to instruct another girl she had met in Attawapiskat, whom she had led to the Lord, how to deal with the spirits that were speaking to her about suicide. She taught her what the Bible teaches. Command them to go in the name of Jesus! So this girl did what she was taught, and the spirits left, and she felt peace instead of fear. This victory over a supernatural creature happened at the command of a child after a two-minute Bible lesson by another young girl. Authority in Christ is age-blind.

When these suicidal, or even accidental, deaths occur, it deeply affects many of the other children.

When we first opened the church door and had so many kids with us, they would paint and draw, as kids do, but we were surprised at how many would make pictures of this one girl who had killed herself, drawing her as a butterfly.

We would ask, How did you know her? And they would say, Oh, she was my cousin, or in some other way related, as many are in these smaller communities. And then, as you would walk with the kids, you would discover just how close suicide and death were to all of them. We would be walking back from the store or somewhere, and they would point to a tree and say, "My uncle hung himself on that tree." Or point to a house and say that's where their sister killed herself. And it was so casual. As if it were just a part of life in the north. And sadly, it was. So can God reach in there? Is He able to touch and heal those that have been affected by this most horrible attack? Let me offer the following report as evidence in the affirmative.

It was a Wednesday service and our fourth week in a new community. And as I had learned, there is no need for a watch; you just give the Holy Spirit as much time as He wants, so we were almost into hour four of our service that night, and it was getting close to 11 p.m.

It had been a wonderful time. Many people were getting healed of deep emotional hurts and pains. Much open confessing of faults. Quite beautiful, really, and very calm overall. Like after Jesus spoke to the storm.

But then these two ladies came in. I was sharing, as I was planning on closing the evening, so I was giving a few final remarks. My final remarks are often as long as some people's sermons, so there was a good twenty minutes that these new ladies heard from me. They had sat a couple rows back from everyone else, and the one lady, that I didn't know, raised her hand and asked if she could speak. I didn't see why not; it was such a wonderful night. It was, as Mel Tari called it, *the gentle breeze of Jesus.* So I said, "Absolutely!" Yet she didn't start how I was hoping.

She said, "I've been sitting here for twenty minutes listening to you. And everything you're saying is just making me angry."

When an evening is flowing so well in the Spirit, and then you hear such a thing right at the end of the night by someone who wasn't there for the rest of the night, it makes you question why you didn't feel led to lock the door.

And then she revealed who she was. She was the mother of a girl who had committed suicide. (The one the girls would draw as a butterfly.) And then she went on for her own twenty minutes. She gave a list of tragedies that she had been acquainted with. Her brother's suicide. Her parents died tragically. On and on. And then she said, "If God promised to be with us... how could He let my baby die?"

And then she stopped. She stared at me with such a stern, angry expression, the likes of which I had never seen. She had come to challenge Heaven. To challenge the goodness of God. As she was sharing, the Lord said to Shannon, "This is Rachel." - The prophetic name God had shown Shannon seven years prior in an open vision in our prayer room. And now here she was, weeping for her children.

What is the verse you give to a grieving mother concerning the suicidal death of her daughter? What is the phrase they long to hear? What can affect such a balm for such a wound? At that moment, in myself, I didn't know. But these aren't times for situational response training; these are times for the ministry and comfort of the Holy Ghost. And if you don't have the Holy Ghost and cannot listen to the Spirit of God in such a situation, victory is a thing that will stray far from you.

As she was speaking, the Spirit brought me to a place where he wanted me to challenge her assumption that God is somehow secretly behind the death of these northern, suicidal children. He said to tell her, "I wasn't involved in the death of her daughter."

To be honest, though I knew I had heard God, I was still uneasy in the mood of the situation. Paul did get stoned and left for dead after all. Not everything is pleasant, even in the middle of God's will.

But we didn't go there to do what feels comfortable; we were there to obey God. So when she finished, I said, "Ok. Now I would like to say something to that." And then I started with what God told me to say.

And if there's a verse that one needs to know for such a situation, where we can trust that God will give us the words to speak when we ourselves don't know what to say: Luke 21:15, where Jesus has promised to give us a mouth and wisdom that cannot be spoken against. That is a remarkable thing. And as I saw that promise come to pass, as I spoke to this hurting and angry mother about the true nature of God. And after I told her that God wasn't responsible for the death of her daughter, the conversation went to a place that I would not have thought to go, especially not even knowing this woman at all.

It went directly into the nature of warfare on earth. The war with the devil, and how he is the one who is here to kill, destroy, and to steal children from people. And then, as the Lord gave me the words, I was as surprised to hear myself say, "And it's the parents responsibility to stand in the gap for their children." And then she began to weep. And she began to confess things before everyone present. It was a remarkable thing to witness.

When she had first come in and started speaking, everyone else in the room grew silent and seemed to crawl back into the corners, as if to say, "She's all yours, preacher." But now, as she wept and confessed, they began to stir back to life as they saw evidence that this was only a work of the Spirit of God.

I continued in what the Lord was giving me to say, and he went right through the word, from Genesis to the end, about the war with the devil. In all my thinking, I never would have thought this was what a grieving mother would need to hear concerning the tragic death of her daughter. But, at least for her, it was.

And as the Lord continued to give me a mouth and wisdom, she began to laugh and then weep again, and then laugh some more. It was as if we were watching God unlock her heart, like a combination lock. A little weeping to the left. A little laughter to the right. And he was unburdening her heart as He went on. This continued for about 20 minutes as well. And then, with tears of joy coming down her face, I said, "Let's pray for you now."

So, in the north, there are many stray dogs. And you will run into some of them as you go on your walks through town, but when I went to pray for her, as I said the first words of the prayer, the church building was surrounded on both sides with dogs barking wildly and scratching at the walls to get inside. That was not something that had ever happened!

If spirits can get into pigs, they can get into dogs. As I prayed for this mother, the dogs got louder and louder, and then it just burst from me, “I bind these lying spirits in Jesus’ name!” And instantly the dogs stopped. There was an eerie calm.

Another fellow who was there with us seemed most astounded by the instant quietness of the dogs. “The dogs!” he whispered excitedly.

And soon after this, the prayer was done. It wasn’t a long prayer. Just sealing in what the Lord had done for her heart. And that would have been good enough. But God always exceeds our imaginations. She looked up at us and said, “While you were praying, I heard God speak to me.” She heard God audibly, with her own ears. He said, “I want you to trust me.”

What an awesome God we serve. To take such a situation and to turn it around in just a few moments. To take a soul filled with deep pain and questions and anger, and to be able to comfort, deliver, and heal in but a few moments. Awesome is the only word for that quality of work. That is our God!

She hugged us and laughed some more, and we gave her a new Bible, and she left, filled with joy, a return to the Lord, and a hope restored. The soul-crushing work of the devil, destroyed by the power of the Holy Spirit.

She told us after that she had been planning to go to Bingo that night, but it had been cancelled. So she and this lady were just driving around town. When she drove past the church, she said it felt like a giant hand grabbed their pickup truck and turned it around, bringing them back to the church.

God knows his business.

Chapter Fourteen

Eagle's Eye View

The power and reality of God was not reserved for the past and the future. God is an ever-present help in times of trouble. Where sin abounds, grace does much more abound. And what is God's grace? Well, when Paul was going through a hard time, he got a revelation directly from Heaven when God said, My grace is sufficient for thee, for my strength is made perfect in weakness. 2 Corinthians 12:9.

Grace is God's strength working on your behalf. It is when God does something for you that you have no power or ability to accomplish in the natural.

As Paul said, after this revelation, he took pleasure in necessities and in distresses for Christ's sake, for in those places he saw the power of God manifest. He learned a secret—that it's truly not by might nor by power, but by God's Spirit!

The body of Christ needs to get back to the Bible way of trusting in God alone. If it doesn't happen by

God's Spirit and power, it shouldn't happen. How many ministries do things in their own effort for meagre results, rather than relying on the life of God within them, working through and for them?!

When we landed in our first northern community, you could see the destruction of sin. What did we do? Quickly develop programs and systems to deal with the natural? No. Because unless you change hearts, nothing really changes. Unless the Spirit changes lives directly, there's really no point in doing anything. We gave ourselves to prayer. We knew we needed to exchange our power for His. And as soon as we did that, God began working and connecting. And when a door was opened, we would walk through it. We made sure our faith had action.

So far, we've shared a few things God did: miraculous healings in the hospital, food multiplying, money appearing and angels singing, children having visions of Jesus, and even God speaking audibly to heal a broken heart. What amazing things God will do for us when we rest in him! When we enter the real realm of faith. But we must always remember, God is no respecter of persons. What he does for one, he will do for all. All he requires is faith!

When people show up because angels are singing over your church, you know you're involved in something that is beyond you. You're in that heavenly flow of the river of life. But we aren't preaching angels. We're preaching the word. We're preaching the cross. But God does confirm his word, with signs following.

On our next trip back to Attawapiskat, it seemed there were many instances like this. Even in the church. People would hear singing from behind them and turn around, and no one (that they could see) was there. And God would just draw in people for a night or two to get saved or healed. There seemed to be many "now or never" moments.

In 2018, when I was preaching five nights a week, one lady showed up at church in the second week. I'd never seen her before. She came in boldly and sat in the front row. She looked like she wanted something.

Me and George, the translator, had really hit a nice stride by this time, and he would even mimic my actions as I'd preach. People were getting hit with a double dose—English and Cree. Both barrels of the Holy Ghost.

I finished my message. People came forward for prayer. A lady with clogged arteries came up. Her doctor had said it wasn't good. They were going to have to do some serious surgery or she would die. Well, after hands being laid on her, she came back the next night after seeing the doctor the next day. She was totally clear and completely healed. The lady who had sat down in the front row watched a few folks get prayer and then left after I prayed for this lady's artery issue. She herself didn't come forward for prayer. I thought, *Well, I guess she got what she thought she needed.*

But the next night she was there again, right in the front. That night the Holy Spirit had me preach a hard message on personal persecution—being excluded from your family if you follow Jesus. How your parents and siblings can mock and persecute you. How the community you live in can turn against you. I preached a message that if you weren't a Christian, you might think, "You know... I think I'll go get a milkshake instead."

But that night, when I gave the altar call, that woman came down and received Jesus as her Saviour. That was the kind of Christianity she wanted to be a part of. She wasn't afraid to follow a Christ where there was a personal cost. Now that's a real decision!

And making decisions to come to an unpopular church is not always the easiest. And where the Spirit is allowed to move is always unpopular with the world, the flesh, and the devil! Even the kids, those friends with our kids, could be mocked and attacked just for mentioning they were coming to our church. One such incident happened to a friend of Alaya's. We've asked her to share it in the following chapter.

Chapter Fifteen

Beauty for Ashes

Sasha was one of the most beautiful people I had ever seen! She had a very cheeky sense of humour that would always make me laugh. Even though she was only thirteen, she could have easily passed for sixteen. Many of the girls in Attawapiskat appeared much older than they really were.

I met Sasha on July 29th, 2018, just nearing the tail end of our second time there. I was hanging out on the church porch with a couple of friends one night as Sasha just happened to be walking by. My friends called her over, and she was with us almost every day after! I was happy to have a friend my age, and we bonded quickly.

A few days later, on August 2nd, as the sun was setting, Sasha, Audrey, Melissa, and I walked over from the church to the gym next door to use the washroom since there wasn't one in the church. When we got there, Sasha's aunt was in the arena watching her boyfriend play hockey with Sasha's uncle.

I waited with the other girls as Sasha chatted with her aunt. She couldn't have been more than twenty-five, with messy hair and raggedy pyjamas. I remember there was something about the look in her eye that unsettled me. Something I called "the evil eye."

They talked for about five minutes. Her aunt tried to get her to stay and watch her boyfriend play, but Sasha told her she couldn't.

"Why?" her aunt asked. "Where are you going?"

Sasha raised her hands and said with enthusiasm, "To church!"

"Which church?"

Sasha looked at me. "What's it called?"

"Faith Chapel."

"Faith Chapel."

"The little white one?"

Sasha nodded. "Yeah."

Immediately her aunt's tone of voice shifted from neutral to harsh. "That's a stupid, dumb church—don't go there."

Sasha didn't reply, just pushed her aunt away from her and headed for the door of the arena. Me and the girls followed her. So did the aunt, repeating what she had already said with just as much force.

Next thing I knew, her aunt gave Sasha a hard shove, knocking her into me and the wall. We filed quickly outside, and that's when the fight broke out. Sasha and her aunt were leaping on each other's backs, pulling at clothes and hair, arms swinging. I wanted to do something but didn't know what. Had I been older, I would have stopped it. But I was so young, and I had never seen anyone fight in person before. I remember how plain and undisturbed the expressions of the other girl's faces were as it was happening, as if they saw this every day.

In an instant, Sasha's face turned bright red, and she started to scream and cry. Her aunt only mocked her for crying and threw cuss word after cuss word, telling her that she was ugly, worthless, and adopted. The whole fight was ugly, but it only lasted a few seconds. The aunt went back inside the arena, cursing. Sasha leaned against the wall of the building, breathing heavily. I stood by her with the other girls, who still looked completely unfazed.

"Are you ok, Sasha?" Audrey asked. After a few seconds, Sasha straightened up and said, "That's why I hate my f-ing life." She walked away crying, and we followed her.

There were several abandoned trailers near the back of the arena. Sasha sat down on one of the steps, her face buried in her hands. I asked if she was okay. She didn't say anything, just nodded. A few minutes passed in total silence until we realized that we all still needed to use the washroom. I wondered how Sasha was going to go back into the arena with her aunt still there after such a fight, but she just pulled her hood over her head and headed for the door. Her aunt was sitting on a bench in the hall, exactly where we needed to pass. She looked up at Sasha as she walked by and began mocking her all over again, calling her a cry baby and shouting more lies about how she was adopted. Sasha told her to f-off and punched her way into the washroom.

This kind of behaviour from an aunt was something I had definitely never seen before. After we had all used the washroom, it was time to leave for good. Her aunt continued to cuss Sasha as she passed, as if it were her new favourite thing. Right before we left, Audrey called her the "B" word and finished by saying, "I hope you get hit with the puck!"

There was an old, broken Zamboni parked outside the back of the arena. Sasha gave it a hard punch on its side and jumped up to sit on top of it. We climbed up after her, all of us keeping quiet for the first few minutes.

I remember that hollow feeling of wanting to say something to her but not having a clue as to what. We were all just kids. Audrey and Melissa were even younger.

Sasha pulled out a lighter and lit a cigarette. She said that smoking made her feel better. Melissa laughed and said, "Did you hear what Audrey said to your aunt? That she hopes she gets hit with the puck?!"

Sasha smiled. "Audrey's always got my back."

"Is your aunt always mean to you?" I asked her.

"No, not all the time," she replied, quietly singeing one of the strings on her hoodie with the lighter. "Sometimes she gives me smokes."

She then told us how her hand hurt from punching the Zamboni.

A little while later, Audrey spotted my mom coming towards us from the church and said, “The mom’s coming!” Sasha quickly put out her cigarette.

“Girls, church is ready!” she told us, and we headed over. It took some time, but gradually Sasha came back to her usual self.

That night, as me and my family were walking back from church, I told Mom about the fight between Sasha and her aunt. Mom began to tell me how it was the demons in her aunt that manifested in response to Sasha coming to church and how what she experienced was called ‘persecution’. When I remembered the evil look in the aunt’s eye, it was easy to imagine her filled with a demon.

Sasha came around every day after that, and when it came time for us to leave a few days later, she was one of the girls to wave us goodbye at the airport with a big, beautiful smile on her face.

I followed her on social media over the years and watched as she gradually involved herself with less and less good things, and I often prayed for God to protect her. Then one night, I had a dream. Me, Sasha, and Mom were riding horses together in a sunny green forest. Sasha was very quiet and going through a hard time. Me and Mom started to talk to her about God, and slowly she started to open up and receive freedom. I watched as she began to talk to her horse, telling her some of the things she was going through, and it made me so happy to watch! God was healing her heart.

The dream felt like a foreshadowing to the future, and I'm still waiting for it to happen! To experience, hopefully, hundreds of days just like that dream, when not only Sasha but *all* young people come into the light of Jesus and experience freedom! When all the ashes are finally turned into beauty. Isaiah 61:3.

Chapter Sixteen

Angelina

One of the benefits of being in an area over many years is that you get to see the paths of people beyond an initial experience. Shannon saw many paths of youth go from darkness to light, but to illustrate the seriousness of things and how quickly you must learn about the hardships and warfare, I think this is perhaps one of the most illustrative that she'll share:

Reading over my Attawapiskat journal takes me back to the very smell of the place, but at the same time, as I read my own words, I think to myself, "Did all this happen to little me and my little family?"

It was all such an adventure in God that I find myself being wowed and blessed afresh every time I crack open that old purple journal and read about what God did on one of the most hurting and deprived reserves in Canada through a family that simply responded to an article we read in the newspaper.

Truly when you pray, like Isaiah did, "Here am I, Lord, send me"—Oh, he will... and it will change your life!

I want to tell you about a girl named Angelina. But since my journal records these events so clearly, I thought why not just copy these entries word for word, so that you, the reader, can experience them with the first impression account in which I wrote them in the evenings when I had a moment to sit down with the mosquito coil burning like sweet incense and the experiences still fresh and tingling.

Day 6

July 2, 2016

So far behind on this. Every day since we made contact with the kids has been so busy that I think it will be impossible to record everything.

The next day, bright and early, there's a knock on the door. It's Melissa and her sister Aria. We soon realize that this is how it will be from now on and thus must be up early—prayed up, dressed, and breakfast. So we went to the store with the sisters and met up with Shania, who was on her way to our place. So we all went over to the Northern Store together.

Prices are jaw-dropping. $12.00 for a box of cereal! $32.00 for flour! Ethan is constantly pointing at things we'd normally get him—but at these prices we just can't. Things we'd see at the Dollar Store back home—stickers that would be a dollar are $12 here. A pair of kids socks (also Dollar Store quality) are $14. It's nuts!

So we got a few items, and $77 later we started for home with our small entourage of children. One of the girls stole some candy, I'm pretty sure. On the way home, one of the girls saw a bike and just picked it up and started riding it—no concern as to who's bike it was. When she was done, she just tossed it in the ditch. So we all come home and make lunch.

Kids all paint more pictures and play. Knock on the door—it's the woman who came over the first night and didn't say hello. She brought her friend Marilyn and two older girls.

Marilyn is about fifty and very friendly at the first meeting—unlike so many who are so withdrawn when we first get introduced. Big smile, and very happy to meet us.

I introduce myself to the girls and ask their names. Angelina is shy, and I can't quite hear her name, so Marilyn tells me it louder. Then I ask the girl standing beside her what her name is, and she just shakes her head 'no' with a timid smile. I'm told her name is Danny. Danny is very pretty with classic First Nations features. She reminds me of someone, but I can't put my finger on who.

So Aaron and Marilyn talk about photography and cameras for a bit, and while I'm making coffee, the girls—Angelina and Danny—come up to me and stand really close and tell me they are suicide attempts. Knowing how common suicide has been here, it still took me off guard.

I said, "What?"

And they told me how they cut themselves and were a part of the last suicide pact. Not knowing exactly how to respond, my mother-heart just blurts out, "Why?" Danny said, "People tease me and stuff." Wild to think you would consider ending your life over teasing.

I thought these girls were about 15 or 16, but they were only 12 and 13. I told them that if they ever needed to talk to anyone, our door is always open and how precious they are—but as I'm saying this, the little kids are running around me, and it's hard to realize how weighty the situation is. I just wanted to clear the room and make these girls cookies and tea and talk to them seriously.

All I can do at the moment is tell them that the problems you face when you're young seem so big—but that when you get older, you realize that those old problems of youth are simply things you had to overcome, and often, they make you stronger.

As I'm trying to make this connection with them, Danny's cup of juice nearly jumps right out of her hand—like it was knocked out by the demon that hangs out with her. It spills everywhere and on her, and of course she gets embarrassed (which is all a kid who's attempted suicide because people tease her needs), and she walks away while I'm cleaning it up. End of our conversation. My heart goes out to her. I hope to have a chance to make a real connection with her at some point.

During their short visit, Danny would occasionally poke me. I'd turn to look, and she'd say, "Just kiddin'."

Angelina wanted to do a picture, so I gave her paper and stuff to draw with. She drew a tree and some clouds. Later, Danny asked me for a pencil, and I brought her into the supply room and opened a big bin. She said, "Can I take the whole thing? Just kiddin'!" Everything was 'just kiddin'.

I found a really nice art set with sketch pencils and sharpeners and erasers, like the one we got Sonja for her birthday. I said she could have it, and she said she didn't have any art supplies at home. I said, "Now you do!"

So after we talked with Marilyn and had our visit, Marilyn, on the way out, asked if we could do some art with the teens here.

She said that the Catholic Church charges a fee to use their building. Aaron and I were more than happy to say, "YES, come here! We'll totally let you do art here!"

We talked about doing some decoupage; I told her all about it, and she got excited. She told us how she just wants the girls (the high-risk girls, like

Angelina and Danny) to have nice artistic things to do to show them creativity and self-expression. So I am looking forward to this and have already started collecting jars.

After they left, I saw that Danny had opened her art kit but left all the pencils hidden in a bowl with a book over it. This was strange to me since she seemed to like it and said she had no art supplies. I think she is like so many who have a hard time receiving.

Day 10

July 6, 2016

... So we get back here and feel the weight of meeting the medicine man, and I am barely able to catch my breath when two more girls come to the door.

Aaron was on his way to the store when he ran into Angelina and her friend Maria (two high-risk girls). They ask to see me, so I invite them in for tea. Maria is very shy and hiding and won't come in without much coaxing and some chocolate. But eventually she comes in, and she and Angelina hang out around the front entrance and need to be nearly escorted to the chairs to have a seat.

I offer tea, but they like "juice" more (which is what everyone here calls it, but it's really just powdered sugar and water, like Kool-Aid). I give them some chocolate bars and muffins. Getting these girls to have a two-way conversation is quite difficult. I ask lots of questions and get very short one- or two-word answers. I know these are high-risk girls who have attempted suicide already—so I try to just chat with them about life. (What they do in the summer, what kinds of things they are interested in, what they did for the year-end trip, etc.) Maria is very withdrawn—not like Danny though—more in a dark, spooky way.

The day is cold and creepy enough as it is, and I can feel a darkness on these girls that my feeble words can't penetrate. It's not a tea party!

Early this morning, while all the sleepover girls were sleeping, something dark and heavy came to see me. It sat on my chest and made it harder to breathe. I was so exhausted from the previous day and restless night that I didn't take much notice of this demonic presence. I felt it and knew it was a demon—but ignored it. I didn't even remember it until later that day. Now, sitting with these girls who have scars all over their arms buried under their big hoodies, I can feel the demonic presence.

I am prepared to say 'No' to them if they ask for any pencil sharpeners. We were informed by Anna not to give the high-risk girls pencil sharpeners because they get the blade out and use it to cut themselves. This was told to me after I gave both Angelina and Danny pencil sharpeners at their request!

My brain doesn't naturally equate pencil sharpeners to suicide. So I was ready for that and thought about how all the art supplies were in the bin in the office and storage room.

So we talked a bit more, and then Angelina said she had to use the bathroom. Knowing that the bathroom is right beside the office where the art supplies are, I go into the kitchen to have a good view of the office.

I hear that she's running the tap. She comes out of the bathroom rubbing lotion into her hands. I noticed that there was no toilet flush—but don't think too much about it. Other girls have been into the washroom to steal things, so I think maybe Angelina was poking around to take some soap or shampoo. Soon after she comes out of the bathroom, they tell me they are going to go.

Aaron comes back from the store as they are putting their shoes on. They say they are going to do some cutting at the cemetery. Aaron and I both think they mean cutting themselves. (Angelina made a cutting gesture on her arms when she said it)—so again, all I can say is "What? Why?"

She says "cutting weeds, you know." Kind of a twisted joke, since we knew they do go and cut themselves at the cemetery—but Marilyn told us about how she has been keeping up with the lawn work at the cemetery and sometimes she gets the girls to help.

But after the girls leave, that comment stays with me, and I suddenly think about my razor in the bathroom. I was so focused on the pencil sharpeners that I totally forgot about my razor that I use to shave.

I quickly go into the bathroom and look behind the mirror where I keep it. It's gone. I look in the shower—not there. I go through the carry-on that has all our toiletries in it, but I know I took it out and have used it since we've been here, and I'm sure I put it in the cabinet behind the mirror. Then I remember that she didn't use the toilet and that she ran the tap water as soon as she went in—obviously as a sound buffer while she opened the cabinet.

Now I have a crisis on my hands, and I know I have to inform Anna—but I don't have her number. I look for our page of contact numbers and can't find it anywhere. So Aaron goes out to track someone down.

When he leaves, I just feel sick to think about these girls using my very sharp razor to cut themselves on this cold, creepy day. I put on some worship music and just pace around, praying and asking God to help. It's hard to know what to pray for—the situation is so disturbing.

Aaron came back after a while and said he ran into Anna (thank God) and told her. She said she knew where to find the girls, so she peeled off with her truck in that direction! Big sigh of relief. Aaron and I continue to pray and declare the Word over the situation. What an awful day.

Is it any wonder that the enemy would do something of this nature? A suicide pact among children in Attawapiskat is what got our attention in the first place and was the reason we put our normal lives on hold to come all that way and let God use us in whatever way He needed to in order to shine some light on this demonic darkness.

Do you see the plan of the enemy here—coming at us with this counterattack? I remember I was pacing the floor in prayer and telling God, "I didn't come here to help these kids for it to end like this"—the enemy indirectly using something of mine to assist in a suicide. The irony! No, this could not happen.

I prayed against this attack, not only for the girls but also because I knew it was a direct attack against us and our coming to the community. As believers, we need to be aware of how on top of his game the enemy is—all the more reason for us to take our job as Christians seriously and remind him that he's a defeated foe and that victory is ours in Christ.

Day 15

July 11, 2016

... As painful as it is in my soul to see this kind of behaviour from Shania, it's far more disturbing to be told that Angelina attempted suicide again.

The morning after the hard day and razor fiasco, Anna showed up early in the morning. She wanted to know if we found the razor. We said no, and so it confirmed to Anna that she did indeed have mine, and obviously some damage was done to herself by it. (Due to the amount of cutting in the community during this time, the kids could not buy razors or even pencil sharpeners at the Northern Store.) Anna couldn't tell us any details because it's confidential, but she did say that it was an ordeal and she had to get the police involved.

Later on, we found out from Marilyn and Floyd (her husband) that she "did it again." I came right out and said, "Attempted suicide?" Let's just be straight up—to which we were told, "Yes, attempted suicide and flown out for medical treatment."

There is a hospital right here on the rez, so if they are flown out, it's serious.

I shudder to think that the razor I brought here to shave my legs was involved. No one will say how she did it—and I feel too uncomfortable asking—but I think it was with my razor. I just thank God that she wasn't successful in her attempt.

Marilyn also said that her liver is so damaged from so many attempts with pills that she could be going into liver failure—at 13 years old!

God, what do we do? It's all too big a situation for everyone here. God alone—through His body—is the only hope. I need to pray more.

We didn't see Angelina again until Aaron went back that winter for a brief ministry trip with another pastor. He was pleased to report that throughout the duration of their stay, Angelina and her sister were at the church the whole time, sometimes with Marilyn and sometimes on her own accord, and had received much prayer and time in Godly counsel and fellowship—even playing the drums during worship! When Aaron told me this, I was so relieved to know that Angelina was doing better and that her heart was ready to receive from the Lord, who is the God of all comfort and the one who sets the captives free (2 Corinthians 1:3-4 and Luke 4:18).

It's important to note that this was our first real mission trip, and even though we were ready and willing, and certainly not babes in Christ; nevertheless, that level of demonic was new and startling. When these girls arrived at the church that day, I thought they genuinely wanted to visit and connect with us. But the enemy is like a roaring lion, walking about, seeking whom he may devour. (1 Peter 5:8)

Whenever you go into the enemy's territory, you must be aware of this and always be ready for the ways in which he'll creep in and start roaring. Paul reminds us not to be ignorant of his devices. Likewise, don't be naive either, but rather expect him to put up a fight. But don't let that stop you! Know this—that if you're in Christ, then you're on the winning side! "But thanks be to God, which giveth us the victory through our Lord Jesus Christ." (1 Corinthians 15:57)

I may not have been expecting this ambush, but thankfully we knew enough to stand on the promises of God and declare that "No weapon formed against me shall prosper." (Isaiah 54:17). Even though he tried to, the enemy wasn't able to destroy Angelina that day!

Day 10

July 20, 2018 (*two years later.*)

Sunny morning. Sitting outside with my tea, Angelina comes by and sits down with me and the kids for about an hour. Two years ago, when Angelina came over to chat with me, it was a set up to get my razor and attempt suicide—but before I was aware of this, it was like pulling teeth to get her to open up and talk with me. This time, she is very talkative and friendly and comes without any hidden agenda or evil plan.

Angelina is a very different girl from two years ago. She is tall and pretty and confident. Unlike the dark, shy girl wrapped in sweatpants and hoodies.

She chats away with us about lots of things: hunting at her family's camp, graduating grade 8 and going to Ottawa for high school, her aunt's dream catchers, how she used to be bullied, cross country skiing and snowshoeing, her dream about Heaven and seeing her grandmother and other relatives there... and she tells us lots of words in Cree.

She tells me about doing the sweat lodge and getting visions of animal spirits and tells me I should do a sweat. It's hard to know how to respond to this, as it's the first time I've really gotten to talk to Angelina for more than a few minutes. I don't want to offend her. I know it takes time to develop trusting relationships here. And though she has experienced some ministry, the renewing of the mind isn't an overnight process.

From her house across the street blasts crazy loud music. This loud music blares all down the street every day, and nobody ever complains about it. Angelina tells me it's her music. She plays it loud in her shed because she says it helps her and keeps her busy. She can often be seen jumping on her trampoline to her terrible, loud rap music. I can't fathom how this can do anyone good, but it's obviously helping her in some way??

Watching Angelina flip all over the place on her trampoline, it's hard to believe that this is the same girl who's attempted suicide so many times that she damaged her liver.

She told me about wanting to go to Ottawa to get an education and get out of Attawapiskat. This would be a good idea for her, especially since just the other day, she and her friends were charged with pushing an old truck into a ditch and setting it on fire! And it was our old beloved rez truck that Jim and Sandra gave to Anna and Alex to use two years ago—and thus we had the privilege of getting to know it. Poor rez truck is now in the "devil's playground"—what they call the junkyard.

Day 14
July 25, 2018

Plan today—see if Angelina will sing on the Stranger song.

This was part of a project in conjunction with the Gord Downie-Wenjack Foundation, where they gave us the rights to use one of Gord's (The Tragically Hip) songs to record Attawapiskat's native youth singing it. In one of the last projects Gord Downie did before he died, he highlighted the plight of the Indigenous youth, in particular one Chanie Wenjack, who froze to death while trying to walk home from the residential school he escaped from. Aaron was asked to be the recording engineer and mixer for the Attawapiskat project, which was then shown in conjunction with the Walk for Wenjack event in Toronto, honouring the legacy of Chanie Wenjack. This also included a large mural made with the Attawapiskat youth, our family, and our friends Marilyn and Floyd, who coordinated this project. This mural highlighted aspects of the community before residential school, during, and after.

Angelina mentioned to me the other day, when we were sitting on the porch, that she liked to sing. So I asked if she'd be interested in singing on the recording.

She said, "Maybe, if I'm not too shy."

I told Aaron, and he messaged her about it, and she said, "Sure!"

This would be great for Angelina—an Attawapiskat youth who's attempted suicide multiple times—to sing on the reconciliation project!

She told Aaron what time she'd be by, so we wait. Still no Angelina. Eventually we see her out on her porch. Alaya calls to her. She says she's too shy. Most of the kids are shy here; they just need to be encouraged. Alaya goes over to Angelina's house, and soon enough, I see them walking back here together. Yea, Alaya!

So Angelina sings! Very quietly though. But at least she did it, and Aaron can do a lot with her voice to enhance it.

That same night at church, Aaron plans to preach on salvation. Before he starts, while worship is still going, Bernice and her mother Lois come into the church. Lois was walking—not in her wheelchair.

Lois is 87 and has been in poor health, but tonight she was feeling good and felt like walking. Bernice excitedly came to the front and told everyone that just a few minutes ago she was on her porch, and she heard angels singing over the church! Her mom came out and heard it too. Just then, Bernice's brother pulled up in his truck and asked them if they wanted to go to church.

During worship, before they came in, I kept feeling like someone was standing beside me. Every time I'd open my eyes to see who it was, there was nobody there—that I could see, but I could certainly feel. Then Bernice and Lois came in and shared their testimony of hearing the angels sing.

How fitting that on the same day that Angelina sang the song—that night the angels were singing over the church!

Chapter Seventeen

Procession

For those initial years, I would say we were functioning as a ministry of helps, such as we see Paul mention in 1 Corinthians 12:28. Whether it was in our apartment, where we'd open it up to homeless drug-addict youth, or whether travelling 6000 km to plant a church in the Yukon, when there was a call, we would help. And honestly, I don't know if you ever really leave that, as that was essentially the same call Paul received from the man of Macedonia. "Come here and help us!" That's all people really need—help. If they're sick, they need help to be healed. If they're suicidal, they need help to see hope. If they're hungry, they need help to be fed.

And so naturally, the more you do, the more the Lord starts to reveal to you different ways that your help can be more effective. And as your sword gets sharper, he calls you into more serious situations.

The next community that would be opened to us would be Wemindji, on the other side of James Bay. We've been there many times since our first trip back in 2016, and eventually we lived in the community.

During our time there, we would connect with people both north and south of us—in fact, all around James Bay. And we began to notice a pattern when I would teach. It became clear that there was more than just a hunger for the word. There was a desperation. And then when we would talk to other leaders in the region, they would tell us that they were seeing the same thing: the need for solid biblical teaching to help restore the churches.

Teaching, through the scope of Ephesians 4:11, had once been a big part of the foundations of the region, but it has since been vacated. It is not the same as preaching or "sharing" a message. The Teacher is a divine gift given by Jesus. All can teach. But when a Teacher teaches, the word hits harder and deeper due to the function of the office.

When we were in Whitehorse, Yukon Territory, we heard how there was a mighty move of God in the 70's among the Klinket. It seemed God was just sweeping people into the churches and training and releasing them on a grand scale. We heard similar reports in Northern Ontario and Northern Quebec from around that time period. Now the need has arisen again. It's a new generation that needs what the last generation enjoyed so much from others: the spirit and the truth.

Now, some churches in these regions do have good Bible-teaching pastors, but many communities do not even have a pastor or even a proper place to meet. So as our time in Wemindji became more regular, God shifted us from simply being a *helps* ministry to teaching, as we then had the time to lay a solid foundation of biblical reality. Stone upon stone.

Naturally, it also helps if the people have a hunger and a desire to grow! Well, you have that in Wemindji. There are so many wonderful people there, hungry for the things of God.

Now, even though God shifted us to teaching specifically, we still had to maintain the simple commands Jesus gave to every believer in Mark 16: lay hands on the sick, cast out devils, etc., but the teaching of the word of God had become such a clear and essential need.

I think perhaps the reason that it has been overlooked in this present hour is that many assume that the Bible is being taught. But there is a great difference between someone preaching from a handful of scriptures and someone bringing over 50 scriptures to establish a truth. Not that it's the number that matters, but to understand something, you need to look at it from each facet.

That old word, "doctrine," that you rarely hear in church any more is more necessary than people realise. It is the establishment of a scriptural reality in the core of a person. It is the table of shewbread in their soul. It is the bringing to a conscious level what is in the mind of Christ. And the enemy will fight you strongly on this line. As he said in the garden, "Yea, hath God said?" He hates the word, as it is the sharp sword that is used against him. So let's use it then!

Chapter Eighteen

Wemindji

Wemindji is a Cree community on the eastern side of James Bay, in northern Quebec. It is directly across the bay from Attawapiskat.

Maantaau ayimihaauchimaau means 'Strange Religion Pastor' in Cree. In Wemindji First Nation, that often would refer to me or anyone that would lead the Pentecostal church. Certain folks in town call our church, where the Holy Spirit is allowed to move upon people, strange. Some people want a God that makes you rigid and stiff, like in a casket. But that's not our God! He's alive! And when the Spirit moves, He makes people look alive!

But desperation has a wonderful way of breaking down the wall of what you think is "strange," if on the other side of that wall you can get genuine help, so they often come to the Jesus that still heals and delivers—like Nicodemas: In the middle of the night.

The eastern side of James Bay, where Wemindji is situated, has a long history of Pentecost. There have been tent meetings and evangelistic outreaches going on there for over 50 years. People are familiar with the Holy Ghost. And there's always the complaints from various leaders or activists against the churches. They seem to come in cycles.

But the main issue in the north is not really that you run into these problems with other religious church groups or the traditionalists (never fear those made of dust); it's that the people who come to the churches today are not being sufficiently trained to walk in their function in the body of Christ. They come to church, but they are not often *sent out* from that church. Because when one walks as who the Bible says they are, religion and devils can't stop you!

So few are being taught in a way where they confidently know that they can step into their individual position and calling—into the mission God has given them to do. I know this because when I have taught people from various communities, this is what I hear. They often tell me how they need "this kind of teaching."

Who we are in Christ and what He has done is maybe being mentioned, but not often brought to a point where there is understanding.

In the places we have been, there are some strong preachers. There's very nice people. There's a lot of salvation messages, but there's very little teaching that can move people from milk to meat, which is essentially, inaction to action! It's very often thought (but this is starting to change) that just the man or woman at the front of the church is going to do mostly everything, and that idea isn't one found in the Bible. Christianity isn't a spectator sport.

Yes, it's clear that there is always an initial person who will "go" as Jesus said and "teach the nations," but after this we should see a consistent stream of leaders being raised up and trained. (Catch, train, release.) But there really isn't. Not on the level there needs to be. But by the grace of God, that's what we plan to remedy.

When we see Paul instructing Titus to appoint elders in every city (Titus 1:5), Paul doesn't say *we need to bring a bunch of folks over from Antioch and put them in these positions*. No. Local leadership is the Bible way. Homegrown is always best!

Aside from this, we clearly see that the body, as a whole, is still made up of many parts! If it's just one person doing all the work, that does not reflect a functioning body. Every part is essential, and everyone has a role in the body of Christ. Each one is different, and none can be dismissed as unnecessary. We see this in 1 Corinthians 12:20.

Yes, there are general things all Christians do. And yes, there are leaders. The church should never be some sort of communistic community, like we see in the rebellion of Korah in Numbers 16:3. And yes, people should be proven before they are put in positions, as the Bible teaches in Timothy and Titus, but you don't need to be sitting in a church, living a godly life for twenty years, before you're able to do something for Jesus!

When we first went to Wemindji First Nation in 2016, it was because their previous pastor had left, so there was a void in the church. Another pastor we knew drove us up in the middle of winter to meet the group there, and he actually wanted us to just jump in and take over where this guy left off. But without relationships and trust, you'll never establish anything. You'll just be dispensing knowledge that you *hope* sticks. But when people trust you, they can receive what you're teaching. That's vital. Trust is a bridge between souls.

The issue with this whole "gap" in the chain of teaching is that the leaders of the previous generation really didn't raise up the Joshuas like Moses did. So you have a group of people that want to go into the "promised land," but don't have a Joshua. So all they've got is a map, and it's a great map, but they don't know how to read it. That's actually where teachers come in.

Now, I'm not going to go too much into their role fully, but I will say that the Ephesians 4:11 teacher is partly designed for crisis situations, which is often where God has sent us. Even on our recent way to Wemindji, we stopped off in North Bay and were again asked about reaching out to a community in Saskatchewan that had lost their pastor, and so the church splintered.

You see, teaching is what connects one to the foundation of Jesus Christ that is in your spirit. It is like the steel reinforcements that run from the foundation to the rest of the building, stabilizing the structure in the soul of the individual and, by extension, the church as a whole.

This is evidenced predominantly through Paul's writing to the churches. Paul says plainly that he is a "teacher of the gentiles," and we see the majority of his teaching came in times of crisis—to gird up the church so that it might not topple over. This is more the work of a teacher than an apostle. Which is why Paul never laid aside his call as a teacher. 1 Tim 1:11. His "right" to teach the specific church simply came through his apostleship as a "father" by being the one that established the assembly. And part of his work as a "father" was to make sure the church would be cared for after he was gone. And his instruction to Timothy was to not only teach the people what Paul had taught him, but he was to find people that could teach others as well. Look for teachers! 2 Timothy 2:2.

I remember hearing a very prominent minister who works in the far north sharing about a pastor in a community who was discussing with him the need to find a replacement for him. This man had been pastoring there for fifty years. He was from the community. Yet he was telling this other minister that they needed to send up someone to replace him. Someone from the south. And the sad thing was, this other minister agreed. And soon enough, this pastor died. And to this day, as far as I know, they are still looking for a replacement from the south. There should be, at the very least, a handful of people that could step in and take that position! But pastors are not training people. And the function of the Ephesian 4:11 teacher is grossly neglected. It's not sent by Jesus to just run a Wednesday night Bible study!

I think this is why God has opened many doors for us to teach the word of God in such a way that it can be functionally applied. Pastors may be here to hold your hand, but teachers are here to put a sword in it!

Each church should essentially be a Bible and mission training school of the Spirit. That's what the vision for the early church was. As most churches in the north currently are not this, what is needed is a place to train the leaders from the north to effectively impact their own communities so that they themselves would start to raise up and disciple believers from within the local community to be effective workers for Jesus. The result will be local leadership training local leaders.

Early in the summer of 2017, when we were coming back into Wemindji, we drove past the house of a church member. (This was prior to our coming up to eventually live in the community.) We had just met him a few months before, and we had gotten to a place where he trusted us to deal with serious situations.

He was out on his porch, and he waved to us as we drove past. We had barely gotten our things out of the truck and into the church when he came to get us.

"There's a lady that has devils at her house. Can you come pray?" He asked and told us he'd meet us at the house.

Now this woman and her children had been having open manifestations of devils. Sometimes walking through the house, sometimes sitting at the kitchen table having breakfast. As clear as you see this book, they saw the devils. The spirits in the north are very bold, and they take full advantage of the fact that the First Nations have always been a very spiritual people and open to this realm.

Just recently, as I was back up in the community, I was called to cast a devil out of a house, and as I came through the door, what looked like a black cat ran out, but then it vanished in the daylight. It's a different place up there. And so we dealt with the spirit and led a man to the Lord in the process.

When we finished getting everything out of the truck, we headed off to find this woman's house. When we pulled up a few minutes later, we found the church member on his phone, pacing around outside. As I got out of the truck, I overheard half of the conversation. He was talking to an evangelist he knew in some other town about the situation. The evangelist was trying to give him some over-the-phone instruction.

And now this is what I mean by a break in the chain of teaching. Here you had a Pentecostal church that had a pastor for years, but he hadn't taught them what to do in such a situation. And it's a very common situation. He hadn't taught them that even if you anoint a window and a door, devils can go through walls! Hadn't taught them how to use the weapons of their warfare so that people might be set free and not tormented by some creature that's so dumb it tried to fight God and his heavenly army!

I personally think one of the reasons leaders are not teaching people the practical side is that it's some sort of job security issue that has crept into people's minds. If the pastor teaches people how to do things, there's less for the pastor to do, and he isn't the star of the show anymore, or perhaps he fears he might lose his priority over others if he's not the only one that's allowed to do things.

But then, there are *some* that simply haven't been taught, so they don't know what they don't know. However, we're in a war, and the enemy doesn't have mercy on ignorance.

One time, an old pastor came to church and heard me teach on healing. Afterwards, he asked for prayer so that he might have faith for healing. He didn't have the faith for it because he himself was never taught properly. But when he heard the word, he knew he needed it! Faith cometh by hearing, and hearing by the word of God. Romans 10:17. This is the sad reality of the broken chain of transmission. The power of the gospel should have never left. But if the word isn't preached and taught, people can't have faith in what they have never heard.

So we went inside and met the woman who called for us to come. She shared with us what was going on, how openly these devils manifested themselves, and also how she had terrible nightmares. Well, we prayed in Jesus' name, took authority over those foul creatures, and left. Later that week we heard back that all the manifestations had stopped, and she had slept wonderfully since we prayed, with no nightmares. That is the God we serve!

And as for that man who was on the phone with the evangelist, he is a solid brother in the Lord and is asked to preach and share in many communities, and it is a joy to see him established in the faith and confident in his position in Christ. He's learned how to work with the Spirit.

I think in many ways we quench the Spirit when we try to be "professional" rather than simply available. Real faith has a ruggedness to it—a simplicity. It is excellent, but not worldly. And when you trust in God, sometimes all you need to do is turn on a light for the Spirit to start working!

Another time, it was getting into early evening, so I thought, *Well, I'm just going to put the church lights on and turn on the outside light as well.*

Within a few minutes of my turning on the light, people started showing up. Pickup trucks pulled into the parking lot. One and then two, then a couple more, then another one. And men as well! Men hungry for a touch of Heaven.

"What's going on?" they would ask.

Not knowing what was really going on, but being aware of how the Holy Spirit moves, we said, "Come in! We're going to have a meeting." And so a couple of us grabbed some guitars and started to sing, and as others joined we all sang and shared a bit.

The Holy Spirit was just demonstrating how easily he can pull things together. It's nothing for God to set up a service.

And then, as we were worshipping, an unknown man came in. He wasn't from the community. He came up to me and asked, "What's going on here?"

“We’re just having a meeting. God has brought the people,” I told him. “What are *you* doing here?” I asked.

“Well, a few days ago I was 400 km from here, praying in the woods, and God came to me, and he called me to be a pastor. I was just driving by and felt to come here. What’s going on here?”

He was in a Holy Ghost daze. God brought him 400 km out of the woods to the church that night, when there was no meeting planned... but God knows his business. He planned one. So we prayed for this man, and God blessed, having words for him, and he went on his way.

Sometimes all you need to see God move is a willing heart and a light switch. We must always remember that it is God’s plan to reach the lost. It is his plan to build his church. It is his plan for the gifts and power of the Spirit. We don’t need to twist his arm to see him work with us. He’s more willing than we are!

We were casting devils out of a house just a couple weeks ago and seeing people baptized and restored to the Lord, and though I would love to share everything—like a group of schoolchildren we would see regularly all getting saved (that was a good day), I think we shall keep with a couple key instances to show the scope of the power of God and how He is truly able to save to the uttermost.

Might the reader be encouraged to take on challenges that are far greater than what they are naturally able to conquer, but to know that through God, we shall do valiantly: For he it is that shall tread down our enemies! Psalm 60:12.

Chapter Nineteen

Jail Time

It was the first time that I'd had an opportunity to go to the local jail in this one community, and it would end up being the one experience that has been burned into my heart. But like in so many instances and testimonies, there's often, in some way, a weaving of youth and children through most of them. God loves families.

Before I went to the jail, we had met one of the local kids who would occasionally come out to church and tell us of his dad. How his dad wasn't around. And when he was, he was nervous around him due to his drinking. He had no real relationship with his father.

But God comes to restore families. To break through the bondage and hindrances that keep them from loving each other and to restore things that many think are beyond repair. This was such a case.

The day started with our Sunday morning service. My message was on vision. How in the Bible, when God gives visions, it's not just so someone can have a spiritual experience; it was used most often to propel them forward into some specific action. When Peter was in a trance on the roof and saw a vision, what was the result? Telling people he sees visions? No. Putting out a book on vision interpretation? No. It led him to a man and family that needed the gospel. When Paul saw the man of Macedonia, what was the result? A direction, an action towards preaching the gospel.

Visions are for the very same reason our eyes are in the front of our heads: to move us forward into purpose and destiny.

So I taught on this, and then at the end of the service, a lady asked if we could pray for her son. He was in the local jail. As we prayed for him, Shannon was given a vision. She saw this man in his jail cell. There was a black door that was moving closer to him. And then she saw a small window appear in the upper corner of the cell. Light was streaming through this window. She instantly understood that there was going to be a window of opportunity for this man, but if he didn't take it, the darkness would consume him. Shannon shared this with the mother.

After service, there is always lingering. Lingering, which sometimes includes a meal, but if not a meal, always coffee and Holy Ghost Bannock.

Holy Ghost bannock is like normal bannock, which is a traditional native bread that is cooked so many ways you can't actually say, "This is the way to cook bannock." Some fry it. Some bake it. Some roast it on a stick over an open fire. When Shannon made her bannock from a simple recipe she had found, she was surprised to see how many of the elder women would ask about it. It would become known as Holy Ghost Bannock. And now the recipe for that lives on the church kitchen wall.

So as Shannon and this lady had a casual after-service chat, Shannon suggested perhaps Aaron could go to the jail to visit him. As she was saying this, the mother's phone rang. It was an officer at the jail. They were unable to pick up lunch for her son that day as they were busy and wanted to know if someone could bring him lunch. She looked over at me.

God knows his business.

I picked up his lunch and headed to the jail. What was I going to say? How much time would I get? Would I get any? I knew what I was "supposed" to say, being a preacher and teacher, but there is that wonderful verse where Jesus says he will give us a mouth and wisdom in the moment. How often I've employed it!

When I arrived, the officer seemed confused about who I was. But he let me in, and I waited a few feet from the cell while the officer spoke to James through the hole in the door. When the door opened, I saw a very angry man.

When he saw me, he didn't respond in any way. He turned back to the officer and asked him if they could speak in private for a minute. So off they went around the corner while I stood there, holding a bag-lunch, in front of an open jail cell. What to do? I had no idea what to do. So I just prayed in the Holy Ghost and waited.

About five minutes later, he returned and grabbed the lunch from my hands and put it on his concrete slab bed. He took a few steps towards me and asked boldly, "So why are you here?"

Well, that's the nail, isn't it? Right on the head. He didn't have time for someone who was just wasting his time. Even if he was in jail.

"I'm here for *you*," I said. And then I proceeded to tell him what has been going on and how God brought us. I shared a few testimonies, and he listened. He didn't say anything. He just watched me. He stood in the doorway of his cell, and I was just a few feet into the hall. I then felt there was space to share the gospel directly. "So, would you like to accept Jesus as your Saviour?" I asked. He thought for a moment. "Naw. I got stuff I've got to take care of." So it was a no.

But... he didn't ask me to leave. So, as a preacher does, I just kept talking. And as I did, I noticed that wonderful river began to move. That river of living water that does things we can never do in our strength. My words became His words. I began telling James that he was here for a purpose. And when I said that, he said, "I always wanted to know what my purpose is."

And so I shared the gospel again, but from the perspective of purpose. How our purpose is to know God, and this is only possible because of what Jesus did, and then all things in our life will flow out of that relationship that Jesus has made available. The access only his blood could give. Where now, we can come home. Home to the Father, who is love.

As I shared, this man, this hardened man, began to tear up. "Now," I said. "Do you want to accept Jesus?" He was rocking back and forth. "Yes," he said. "But I need someone to teach me."

I said, "Let's pray," and with the officer looking on just a few feet from us, hearing everything, I took his hands, and we prayed in front of that jail cell. And wouldn't you know it, that man walked into the light of salvation that came through the window of opportunity Shannon had seen a little over an hour before.

When I took him by the hands, he would later tell me that he felt power, like electricity, shooting through his body, from his feet all the way to the top of his head. He said it made him feel clean. He wasn't a Pentecostal. He didn't know the "lingo." He didn't know people talked about the power of God like electricity. He just knew that he prayed with me, and this was his experience. He had struggled with hard drugs for 14 years and spent much of his life battling alcohol addiction. But that was behind him now. He had also been involved in supplying substances to several prominent figures in the community. But that, too, was now in the past.

He gave me a huge hug, and then the officer came over. I had to leave, but we made plans for me to return the next day. And so I did.

We met for the next 12 mornings. The first day I brought him a Bible. We would have coffee and do a Bible study, sometimes for 2 hours, depending on what officer was there. Some would let me sit on a chair in his jail cell doorway. Others, the door had to be closed, and I would teach through the hole in the cell door. But in all that time, he never had one symptom of withdrawal. The Lord delivered him completely and healed him from any negative effects of many years of substance abuse. He had also been tormented with nightmares. These also stopped immediately.

He would write about those days being not time he spent in a jail cell, but in a classroom. He was a new man. It was amazing to see. The Bible studies were not "new believer" level of teaching, as I didn't know if any day would be the last day I'd see him before they ship him south to a larger jail. You never know when. So I taught him the highest form of Christianity I could teach. The victorious gospel. Not the dead postmodern Christian fluff that's taught so often today.

He didn't need to know that he was OK and I was OK. It was the triumph of Jesus, lived through His church, that he needed! It was power and not just words. And wouldn't you know it, when Heaven declares you're free and justified and that someone paid the penalty for you, the strangest things can happen. At the end of those 12 days, all the charges against him were dropped. He was released.

Two weeks later we would baptise him in water at the church. His salvation shocked many. His mother and father had the first conversations they'd had with their son since he was eleven years old. It was the Lord's doing, and it was marvellous in our eyes.

His son would tell us soon after that his dad was a different person. They spent time together and talked. They had never really done that. He wasn't afraid of his dad anymore, and they would come together to church every Sunday. Truly, the Lord gives us a new heart!

I want to include his testimony as recorded at a special meeting we had shortly after his release. He is sharing about his time in jail and when we first met. This testimony is taken from an audio recording.

"When I... when I went to the... jail... thirteen, thirteen days ago, I was angry. I was very angry. And...when I went there, I expected to get and to have discomfort, withdrawals, and bad dreams. I always had bad dreams. And I said, There is nothing good that's gonna come my way. Nothing will ever, nothing good. I said, Ok God, send me your worst. I was willing to take a challenge. And the next day, he sent a white man to deliver food to me.

Then when we first... when we met, and I told him about it. Like, and I also told him the things that I had done that I had succeeded in my life that I am proud of. Like, I had all kinds of work experience. I had welding. You know, becoming a miner. And I told him, There's... I have a...I feel hollow... that there's something empty inside me; I needed something, I want something, I need to be fulfilled. He told me, You need, that's Jesus. I believe that. Then he told me a lot of things, you know. He... then... I decided to ask him... teach me, teach me. Teach me he did. We did a, a sinner's prayer. When we did that sinner's prayer, I felt something right in the middle of my heart... that was cracked. I felt the energy flowing through my body. It was the Holy Spirit. It was so pure. I cried. I'm never gonna forget that feeling. The love of Jesus Christ is pure. And His presence, you can feel it... I slept."

The night he shared this testimony, the officer that had arrested him was at the meeting. With his gun on his hip, he came forward for prayer.

God knows his business.

Once news of what happened at the jail began to spread, I was called to the police station to meet with the current chief. He let me know he had heard about what happened and that he appreciated it. Another officer had also heard about this event. This would lead to a rather humorous situation that I'll share at the end of the book. But when light hits darkness, it affects so many more than just one person. It affects all who know that person.

So what do people like this need now? They need to be trained. They don't need to just go to a church and hear a nice message and walk with people that aren't going all in for Jesus.

It is more essential than ever to have churches that are on fire for the Lord and are able to equip the people and can do the work of the ministry! It is good for people to encounter God in a strong way to get them in the Kingdom, but that strength needs to continue, and especially for those who were serious in serving the devil, they need to be working for Jesus, or their minds can wander into religious ditches!

The churches need to know how to disciple and raise people up. It is now, more than ever, time to be bold and fearless in our proclamation of the gospel in the darkest of places.

Chapter Twenty

Dinner and a Shaman

It's not every day that you meet a Shaman. But when you do, it's never boring, of that you can be sure. Shaman are also called Medicine Men, or Healers. The first Shaman we had met was in 2008 in Alberta. A man named Adolphus Kootenay. He had come to preach and share at our tent chapel services, and it was a great honour to meet him. He was, at that time, a very saved preacher. He had been a Shaman for years and had done many strange and horrible things until he met a power greater than the devils he served. That power's name was Jesus. He had written a book about his path out of, what he called, the Indian religion.

We had, coincidentally enough, read this book the week before meeting him. It was a full expose on life behind the rattle and shaking tent. The book is called *Out of Bondage*. He shared how he entered Shamanism, his training, the things he would do, and his deliverance from it. There is no book like it that I know of. And I would say it is a mandatory read for anyone wanting to delve into this world. Ignorance is not a fruit of the Spirit.

We had also met a Shaman on our first trip into Attawapiskat in 2016. He would call to us one day on the road and tell us that he knew us. Spirits tell them things. He would generally keep away, and we only had occasional dealings with him, except for a brief moment Shannon had on the church porch where he argued his point that his spirit and Jesus were spirit brothers. To which Shannon was quite firm that there was no possibility of that!

One day, in another community, I was invited for a chat. It was February. I had been pastoring the church there for a few months already, and there was a great swell of joy and excitement in the people as they saw healings and deliverances and wonderful things from Jesus.

In our previous November camp meeting, while the service was going on, a call came to the church. A young man had shot himself in the chest with a rifle. He was found bleeding in the snow. So they called us to pray. And we did. And Jesus answered. The young man would live. It was a true miracle. And after the one key drug dealer was saved and baptised in water, people tore the roof off of what God could do.

There is so much benefit to all when an entire body of believers embraces the unlimited potential in God. As there is no situation, no circumstance, no pit too deep, no person too far gone that He cannot reach.

And so it was: the man who had been gloriously saved in prison was on the other end of the phone, inviting me into a conversation.

He said, "I've been talking to my friend for the last five hours, and he has finally agreed to meet you." Well, when someone takes five hours to decide if they even want to see you, I knew there would be something odd at the end of this meeting, but I didn't know just what. So off I went, over to James' house. He was staying with his parents now. Something they were overjoyed with. They got their son back.

When I arrived, James met me with his new wonderful grin. He had transformed so much from the first time I met him in prison. He welcomed me in and took me right over to the kitchen table, where I met Edward.

Edward was a fast talker. I shared for a couple minutes about what God had been doing and being used to such powerful positive responses to the gospel. I was settling in for something similar. But Edward didn't care. Instead, he waited for me to pause briefly, and then he launched into what ended up being a two-hour lecture on the benefits of being a Shaman.

He had three main spirits he would work with. There was the usual, a spirit guide, another spirit he would call his bird, and then one he referred to as his giant. It was like meeting an unholy trio of devils. They would give him information, as familiar spirits do, and they would fight for his territory and they would use him to perform various acts and sacrifices.

Edward shared about a few things he'd done: Travelling through dreams and making people blind, or the usual curses or use of demonic wisdom for financial gain, or the nature of the spirits he served, occasionally they would speak to him mid-sentence, and he would say, "Yeah, they don't want me to share any more with you. They say I've shared enough."

But his desire to gloat over his power would have him sharing more and more. And then his spirits would again tell him to stop sharing with me.

And that was the end of our chat, if you could call it that. And so I said, “Well, it was nice meeting you, but I’ve got to be going,” and I left.

The thing about fishing is, sometimes you’ve just gotta let the fish run. Let the line out a bit. Too often people try to jerk them into the boat.

The next day I kept rolling over in my head how strange the meeting was. I was a little annoyed that I had shared so briefly and the Shaman had gone on and on, though it did sort of feel like he was spilling the beans.

I was just finishing the setup for church that night. No one had arrived yet, and I was at the front of the church. I turned around after setting a guitar on its stand, and there at the back, in the middle of the aisle, was the Shaman. He had shown up at the church. *How strange*, I thought. He gave no signs that he was remotely interested in anything I had to say, and yet here he was, the first person at church that night.

I can't confirm it, but I'm pretty sure I saw a tumbleweed roll by. "Hey Edward," I said, and I went to greet him just as others started filing in the church. He said hello and then just kept to himself at the back, nodding to people as they came in. Most seemed quite surprised to see him there. Then James came in. He was helping someone move earlier that day and had blown out his knee while moving a fridge. He came limping into church, but when he saw Edward there, he let out a loud "Hallelujah!"

Now, James had never gone to a church that taught him the days of miracles and healings are past. He had only done our Bible studies in the jail and then a few services since then. So he was fully convinced that this new Jesus he found would be able to help. He came limping over to me, dragging his leg.

"Aaron! Pray for me!" he said as he told me the story. Well, this got the Shaman's attention, and in no time he was standing next to James, waiting to see what the preacher would do in such a situation. I said, "Ok, let's pray." And I put my hands on his knee and commanded it to be healed in Jesus' name. Instantly, James started jumping up and down. He was smiling and laughing. He was healed.

I noticed that when I was praying, the Shaman moved backwards. When James skipped off to find his seat for the night's service, Edward said to me, "Something came off that."

"What?" I asked.

"When you said *the name of Jesus*. Something came off that."

Edward had felt power emanate and hit him when I said, "In Jesus' name." It pushed him back a bit. That got his attention.

That night, as the Shaman was there, my message instantly changed to preach on the dominion of the believer in Christ. How God has given to us power over devils and all the work of the enemy. If there was a spiritual machine gun, I used it that night. I kept looking back at Edward as I preached. He wasn't running for the door. Interesting.

After the service, he came up to me to ask me about my teaching on casting out devils. He said, "So you, uh, you what... You just... cast them out?"

"Yes. Basically. Come out! Like that."

Edward turned to the side, like someone was talking to him, then turned back to me. "Oh, they really don't like you now!" he said, referring to his devils.

"They better not!" I said.

Edward then, surprisingly, asked if I would pray for him. He told me he can't self-heal. He needs to go to another Shaman for that. His spirits won't do that for him. Well, we found a chink in his demonic armour.

"Of course I'll pray!" I said.

It was something in his chest he couldn't get rid of. So I laid hands on him according to Mark 16 (which is technically believers on unbelievers as it's tied to Matthew 28), so I was biblical, and he let out a roaring cough. And then he felt his chest. The pain was gone. He thought about that for a moment and left.

Round Two: Jesus 1. devils 0.

He would come to church around three more times. And each time he was there, the message would always glorify the mighty power of Jesus. That was intentional. Part of warfare is boasting on your God and diminishing the enemy in the eyes of those that get tangled up with him. They must know there is a difference in power, and it's not even close.

This is why it's such a wretched thing for any church to deny the move of the Spirit. To quench the Spirit. To speak against healing and power as if it's some old first-century idea that is lost in the dust. No. There are situations and people that you will meet when you get into the highways and byways, and these people will not bow their knee to a powerless gospel and a powerless Jesus. If their devils are offering them present power, how dare a church teach that devils have retained their power while Jesus has left the church bereft of any! That is sin. That is a doctrine of devils to keep the church weak and ineffective.

It would be a couple weeks before I would hear from Edward again. He was planning on fighting a Shaman in the south to gain more territory. But he was also liking what he was hearing about at church and couldn't deny that Jesus could do what his own devils wouldn't. He would ask me if perhaps he would be able to use the power of Jesus against that Shaman. I told him, if Jesus is your Lord, there is no devil that is an issue. He was visibly concerned with this potential fight.

Occasionally, if there is a real medicine man with a strong devil, those that challenge them can be killed by their spirits. In another community that I won't be talking about in this book, there are Shaman that can circle cast and can shoot people in other communities through these circles. They are like demonic portals between locations. So if you're in that world and fighting for more territory, it can be a serious fight.

I have often found that some of the most profound moments in this walk of faith come out of ordinary happenings. Things that seem so unassuming soon lead to a passionate discovery of the will and power of God working behind the scenes. This was such a day.

It was mid-March. I was at the church when James called. There was no special tone in his voice. He didn't let on that there was anything going on. He simply asked if I'd like to come for dinner that night.

As I didn't have any formal plans other than our usual meal, I accepted. He then asked if I could pick up Susanne on the way. She was a faithful lady who was at every Bible study and was always eager to learn. I thought it was odd to pick her up for dinner though, but apparently he was having something of a dinner party, or so I thought.

When I picked her up, she jumped in the van, happily clutching her Bible. "I brought my sword!" she said. Why one would need a sword (Bible) at dinner made me even more curious. *She knows something*, I thought. When we arrived, James greeted me just as before and led me to the same table, just as before, and there was Edward, just as before.

It was dinner and a Shaman.

James had cooked Niska (goose), rabbit, and giant dumplings. We all ate. Conversation was strangely quiet. Edward, who was normally gregarious and bold, seemed more tame. Inward. Reserved. And then, as the Spirit often does, he made me know that it was time to focus on the more pressing matter. Body food is fine. But soul food is better.

There are times when you deal with certain individuals that you can't be afraid to boldly confront them. You don't just quietly waltz around darkness; you challenge it directly. So I did.

I said, "Well, Edward, you've come to church these few times, and you've heard the gospel. You know the power of Jesus. You've been healed yourself. You know Jesus is the real God, and what I've preached is true, so now, will you or won't you accept Jesus as your Saviour?!" Edward bowed his head and nodded yes.

I darn near threw those giant dumplings at the wall, climbing over the food to pray with Edward. So I led him to the Lord right there. James and Susanne were bursting with joy. James gave me a look as if to say, *And that's why I invited you to dinner, preacher.* As we were praying, I cast out those devils that had so long held him. (30 years) He was amazed that they were just gone. The power of Jesus is unmatched.

Now, a Shaman will often use objects for various purposes. For Edward, it was his bandana. It was the object he would channel demonic power through. It was his identity, in a way. "Well," he said. "I guess I better get rid of this." So off we went to the dump. And just like another time in December, when we burned one lady's bags full of the devil's spiritual trash, we got ready to burn more.

In December, after a prayer meeting, a lady decided to follow Jesus by leaving behind her native spirituality. She was a jingle-dress dancer and brought bags of paraphernalia to burn at the dump. It is always a joy to see people light that sort of stuff on fire. Just like God said, burn their groves with fire! Deuteronomy 12:3. She was also healed of cancer and other things.

When we got to the dump, Edward put the bandana in a small cardboard box and set it in the snow a few feet from us. As he went to light it, he said, "We should probably stand back." I soon found out why. Though it was just a simple cotton bandana, when he lit the thing on fire, it filled the air with such a noxious fume that one would think we were burning tires. It was acrid and harsh, and I kept reminding myself that it was just a cotton bandana.

If ever evil had a stink, that was it. That bandana burned with a good hot flame. Then we hopped in the van and headed back to town. What a night. What started as a simple dinner ended in a wonderful bonfire of deliverance! And now there was one less Shaman and one more born-again soul.

Chapter Twenty-One

Hands and a Few Healings

The thing about the north, or really, any genuine ministry (the north simply has a more immediate way of moving you into that place), is that your life/time is not your own. It would be wonderful to schedule in advance when people need prayer for their emergencies.

"We will be praying for emergencies between 2-4pm each Thursday." Wouldn't that be easy? But so often, as is the case, the immediate needs are simply immediate. It's you, Jesus, and the trouble right now! I'll share a couple examples here.

One Saturday evening, I was just finishing up mopping the church floor in Wemindji. It was around 10 p.m. when I received a message on Messenger.

"Aaron, there is a boy a family is requesting for healing. 18 years old, I think."

"Ok... Do they want someone to come pray, or do they want us to pray from here?"

“Hold on...to come. To go at his place.”

“Great! When? Can come anytime.”

“Hold on.”

“Tonight, tomorrow after service?”

“Now he says.”

“Ok... Did you want to come then? Two by two, eh?”

“I’m with my little boy atm.”

“Ok. What’s his address?”

And so off I went in the -35 night to find the young man that needed prayer for healing. Thankfully, the house was only a few blocks away.

It was around 10:30 when I arrived at his house. His father opened the door. I’m not sure if he was in his pyjamas, but it was something you normally don’t show to strangers. When I came in, the dad asked me if I wanted a guitar to do some songs. “No. That’s ok. I’ll just pray.”

I came into the kitchen, where the young man’s sister was sitting at the kitchen table eating some late-night cereal and watching me curiously. I also would be wondering why I would be at the house so late. And then the young man walked over.

He had been standing in the doorway on the other side of the kitchen while his mom looked on from a reclining rocker in the living room. He had a very bad skin condition. One of the worst I'd ever seen. His skin was peeling and scaly everywhere. There was no way to hide it. The family was unable to get any help that could manage it, which is why you ask for prayer at ten at night—you're desperate.

"Hello," I said. He just nodded his head. "Well, let's pray and see what Jesus can do," I said, extending my hands towards his. He could hardly hide how embarrassed he was by his condition and wouldn't look me in the eye for very long.

My prayer was brief and to the point, as any command of faith is. Perhaps so much so that the family seemed like they were a little shocked by the brevity. So to help them with this new form of prayer, I added a general blessing over their house and everyone in that room. When people are used to long religious prayers, it can take a minute for that expectation to be renewed to the Bible way of prayer.

And then I left and headed back to the church. When I got back, I messaged the guy who the family had reached out through. "Have prayed for him. He will see Jesus is still real."

A little while after this, that young man showed up at church. I had just finished preaching when he came to the front to share how he had accepted Jesus and wanted prayer. "Why is this fella familiar?" I kept thinking as I prayed for him. Then, at the end of the prayer, I realised who it was. He had been completely healed. No steroids. No creams. No needles. Just the name of Jesus.

God knows his business.

It can be hard for some people to not instantly see the results of their prayer. But you have to remember, healing and miracles are different. Healing involves some measure of time. Whereas miracles can skip right over time and produce the end result. So when you pray, believe in that moment they are healed, as the word says they are, and let the process of the Spirit of life work. We do see many instant healings, which technically would be miracles, but we also see progressive healing. Like when Jesus prayed for that boy who “began to amend.” He got better from the moment Jesus engaged His faith. But it was still a process. John 4:52-53.

It was a similar situation with a man we knew in Attawapiskat. I had been teaching in our Bible study how to cast out devils, and the next day he showed up at the church with half of his face fallen due to a palsy attack. But we would be flying out in a few hours, so Shannon and I got to it and sat him down and blasted that palsy attack in the name of Jesus.

The next time I would see him was when I was preaching. A man came forward and said there were a lot of Cree-only elders at the church that night, and if I wouldn’t mind, he would translate the message for them. Of course I didn’t mind, and he came up on stage with me. It was a great time learning to preach with an interpreter. Essential for every preacher to experience. It causes you to preach in complete sentences and ideas.

At the end of the night, I thanked him for helping, as he must have done a fine job for the people responded well to the invitation for prayer and filled the altar at the front.

When we were walking back to our lodging, Shannon said, "It was nice to see George up there with you."

"George? George who? Where was George?"

"He was the translator for you tonight!"

He had looked so different from the last time I saw him; I didn't recognize him. A couple days after we had prayed, he was completely healed. We were gone before we could see it. When he was translating with me, he looked completely normal. Amazing what God does.

Another lady had severe eye issues, so she came for prayer one night. The following week she would go south to Montreal to the eye doctor. This was her text to me: "*Good news! My eye pressure is back to normal and no eye damage or any disease! It's all Jesus! He's the healer, Amen.*"

Another time, during a week of special meetings, a storm hit. What was amazing is that people drove through the winter storm from various reserves around Wemindji to come for the meetings. The hunger was legitimate. But because of this storm, there was a boy who was in a health crisis and was unable to get flown out of his reserve, so we got a call to pray for him. We did. The next morning, the report came back. "*Off oxygen. Doing good. A miracle turn around!*"

On Feb 14th, this message came through, and I'll quote it verbatim as it was sent to me. Now we, along with others, had prayed for this lady a couple times, as you do whatever it takes to get the victory Jesus has already provided. Sometimes you must press a little stronger through the lies. Mark 8:25.

So she said, "I AM HAPPY TO ANNOUNCE THAT THIS CASE IS CLOSED. NO RADIATION. NO CHEMO. NO SURGERY. NOTHING. Just Jesus and prayer treatment. By the grace of God's hand, it is closed! And this is my Valentine. God's love and mercy! A tennis ball-size mass. GONE. No cancer detected in my body. Me, my fiance, drove out of the hospital celebrating, and me in tears, completely humbled! When she told us the good news, we immediately said, "God is good!". I just want to thank our true healer, Jesus."

This is our Jesus! I would perform her wedding because she was still alive, because Jesus still heals!

And then we have situations that cause laughter; it truly is like medicine. And many times you find yourself in such wonderfully strange situations or circumstances that you just have to laugh, regardless of how it looks.

One day, as I was heading back to church from the store, I was sitting at a stop sign when an officer in his police truck pulled up next to me and motioned for me to put the window down.

"Aaron, I have someone for you," he said. "Can you come by the police station now?" "Ok. I'll just drop the groceries off at the church and come by," I replied, and we both went our ways.

When I arrived at the station to meet up with the officer, he informed me that he had just locked this fella up. He was so excited about what God had done in that jail that he was sure he would do something for this man as well if he could just get Aaron in the cell with him. And so he did.

He opened the jail cell, I grabbed a chair, and sat inside, and then the officer locked the door behind me and headed off into the station. Now, in the 12 days I had met with James, I was never locked in his cell with him. I would usually be at the door with an officer standing around 8-10 feet away. Or if the door was closed, I was seated outside, and we talked through the hole in the cell door. But this one officer had some things to do, so he just locked Pastor Aaron in the cell with this man.

So this man was in his late 20s. He was talking quickly. He sat nervously on the cell's bed across from me and constantly rubbed his legs as if he were washing a shirt in an old washboard tub from the 1800's. What the officer didn't tell me, until later, was that he was brought there because he had assaulted his girlfriend and was currently coming down from a cocaine/and or other major drug high. That's usually information best shared before you get locked in the cell with them.

I shared Jesus with him as best I could, but it wasn't long before it was clear to me that he was still too far gone in his mind. Nothing was sticking. I leaned back to the cell window to see if the officer was there. Nope. He was gone. Well, this was new. Locked in a cell with a violent young man coming down off a drug high. It's moments like that when you can only laugh. I did my laughing inside.

I knocked on the door to try to summon the officer to the cell. No response. Hmm… Fortunately, he had called me a couple days earlier, so I had his number in my cell. I called him. Well, he had decided to just leave pastor Aaron in the cell with the addict while he took a drive around town. “Oh!” he said. “I forgot! I’ll come back and let you out!”

“Thanks,” I responded.

He was there in about ten minutes and let me out of the cell. I did share the gospel to the extent I could, and the young man still thanked me for coming and made a drug-induced promise to come to church and try to be a better person. It’s not everyday you get to experience such a thing.

There’s always amusing situations in the kingdom of God. Another day, as I was also coming back from the store, though this time walking, I passed a house where there were a few folks on the front porch. They were still partying from the night before. They yelled to me when I was around 200 feet away—an interesting distance to start a conversation at, but nevertheless, it started.

"Are you a teacher?!" one of them yelled.

"No!" I yelled back.

"You don't teach at the school?!"

"No!" I replied. Now we were around 100 feet apart and closing.

"When did you get here?!"

"A few months ago!"

"What are you doing here?!"

"I'm pastoring the church!"

"A pastor?"

"Yes!"

"Pray for us!" and they came running towards me and surrounded me at the end of their driveway. As I prayed for them, they solemnly bowed their heads, and then a small group of girls filed out of the house and headed down the road. "Pray for us too!" they yelled over when they saw what was going on. Some of them were led to the Lord right there on that driveway. So it was a whole lot of prayer for these folks that started as a trip to get eggs.

Sometimes it's humorous, and other times it's as serious as it gets right from the outset. But Jesus can always manage it. There was a time recently, during special services, when our church service had reached six hours, and then after the service, a group of us had gone to another house near the church to continue to fellowship and sing some gospel songs. Endurance is vital up there! Those Wemindji brothers and sisters are wild!

As I was preparing to leave, around 2:30 am, one of the ladies from the church leaned over to me and told me there was a family coming over for prayer. They arrived a few minutes later. Their daughter-in-law was suicidal, and they didn't know where she was. So just like Jesus showed us in Mark 7:29, you don't need to be present with the person to deal with a devil affecting them; we dealt with the spirit. How do you know? She was at church the next night and answered the wonderful call to salvation!

And that is often how it is. When you make yourself available at all times for the Lord, you can expect many situations at all times of the day as God weaves your life into the intersection of others who need a word of encouragement, a healing, a powerful deliverance, whatever the case may be.

When the kingdom of God is on the inside, where it is righteousness, peace, and joy in the Holy Ghost, and you are baptised in the Holy Ghost, then you always have the full resources of Heaven at hand. You always have what you need when you need it. It's not because you see it with your eyes, but you, like Moses, endure as seeing he who is invisible. Hebrews 11:27

Chapter Twenty-Two

Ministry in the Last Days

Ministry is God moving through you. Paul says of New Testament ministry that it is the ministration of the Spirit. 2 Corinthians 3:8. At the best of times, it is no longer you that lives, but Christ who lives in you that people will see.

If you want miracles, you must get in over your head. The miraculous demands the impossible. If you're ever in a situation where you think you can do it without God, you're either in the wrong place or the wrong mind. God will never lead you into a place where you don't need the reality of the kingdom. People are literally dying to see someone who serves a living God. A God that is manifestly supreme, clearly more powerful than their troubles, and one who is able to bring about a decisive victory.

A gospel of words alone is not the gospel. 1 Thessalonians 1:5. Our work as the church is a cooperation with the Lord; it is a co-labouring. We preach; he confirms with power. We lay hands; he heals. We pray; he answers.

Always remember, the purpose of prayer is answer, not prayer. We're not Buddhists. We don't pray just to pray as a discipline. We pray because our God answers! He openly mocks people who pray to stones and wood that are dead images and can't hear and can't respond. Isaiah 44:9-12. Our God hears our prayers and responds with might! 1 John 5:14-15. That's what people need to see. They need God. Not pet doctrines—God!

As Paul said to Timothy, preach the word! Nothing else is sharp enough for the task, and in the end, though people may applaud you, they won't remember your catchphrases. Your humour will fade from their minds, and your books will collect dust. So preach the word!

Speak the word only, and my servant shall be healed. That is the understanding of faith. That is a faith that Jesus said he had not found before. One that just sees the value in the power of the word. So value it. It will pull you through when nothing else will. And pray in tongues more than you think you should. You don't always know what you need or how to pray. That's a fact. Often our biggest prayers are still too small. So use the perfect prayer of your spirit, which is one spirit with the Lord.

And no matter what happens—how hard it gets, how loud the enemy barks—never, ever back down. Jesus is the Victory! And he's already given it to you. We're not fighting to win. We're fighting because He already won. Even in the darkest situations, he always causes us to triumph! 2 Corinthians 2:14.

Lastly, a couple key points, and I think they are relevant to any mission work but especially when you are with the First Nations: you are not going into places to change culture. You are going so that people can change kingdoms. There is a difference. You must go low and honour the people. 1 Peter 2:7. Allow for the Holy Spirit to reveal and convict if you come across things that are not congruent with the Bible. He will. We have seen it many times.

Like Proverbs 18:13 says, if you answer a matter before you hear it, it is folly and a shame to you!

There are ways people do things that are not how you do them. It is vital for you to gain understanding before you speak into any matter. Now there are certain things that are obvious, but remember you're fishing. You offer the truth. You demonstrate the Kingdom. There are ways within local cultures that, if you don't humble yourself to understand them, your "mission" can be over before it starts.

We had met a couple self-proclaimed "missionaries" in Attawapiskat who showed up at the church one day and announced themselves as missionaries to Canada. They complained about the people in the town, complained about the dust, and complained about the First Nations financial situation overall. The one woman said, "You know what the problem with them is—too many government handouts."

Imagine being that ignorant and showing up on a reserve, calling yourself a missionary! That's what southerners call "ignorance gone to seed." They were ignorant on every count. We had to pray them out of town so that people would not think they were associated with us.

They even prayed for an elder to heal from being at residential school without even knowing if she had been! They just assumed. It was also this elder's birthday! She did not go to residential school.

And thank the Lord, the elder didn't speak English, so she didn't understand this woman's insane prayer. We did. Others did. The elder's son hid his face in the corner in disbelief while this woman almost spoiled a birthday with an ignorant prayer. So we prayed even harder for them to be removed from the community. They left within a week. Thank the Lord!

Lester Sumrall has an entire course on world missions that I highly recommend for anyone who wants to start reaching farther and wants wisdom from a giant in the faith who offers real-world experience. Don't be a tourist. Be a giant killer.

Chapter Twenty-Three

The Vision

Habakkuk 2

1 I will stand upon my watch, and set me upon the tower, and will watch to see what he will say unto me, and what I shall answer when I am reproved.

2 And the LORD answered me, and said, Write the vision, and make it plain upon tables, that he may run that readeth it.

3 For the vision is yet for an appointed time, but at the end it shall speak, and not lie; though it tarry, wait for it; because it will surely come, it will not tarry.

We are going to build a Bible and missions training camp for First Nations families. The entire family will be equipped so that they themselves can reach their own communities with the sword of the Spirit and the power of God—seeing people saved, healed, and delivered in Jesus' name!

As we discussed at the beginning of this book, the devil's great attack through the government and a false Christianity was to separate the family. To isolate children from parents; daughters and sons from mothers and fathers. But through this camp, God is doing the exact opposite! He is uniting and building up the entire family so that they, as a team, can work together to bring a kingdom-level change to their communities. Fathers, mothers, brothers, sisters, sons, daughters, and grandparents, all working together, united to see the power of the gospel flow like a mighty river! Hallelujah!

First Nations leaders that we personally know will also work with the camp, teaching and sharing their wisdom and expertise with these families. It will be a true cooperative work of the full body of Christ.

At the core of this work will be a local church, as the church is the army of God on the earth. It is the pillar and ground of the truth. And the church has the only true ministry of reconciliation! 2 Corinthians 5:18.

The local church at the camp will run year-round and will be open to all, but the specific training aspects will run four times per year, following the seasons, running a total of 8 weeks each, with one month between them. Each two-month period fully completes the entire initial group of teaching.

1. Winter: January/February.
2. Spring: April/May
3. Summer: July/August
4. Autumn: Oct/Nov

The connection and cooperation with each family that attends the camp will extend beyond their completion of the courses, as we pray for and support their God-given vision for their individual communities. The key purpose of the camp is to establish a core of Biblical truth and spiritual reality within each family that can then be built upon by real-world experiences through walking with Jesus and being a light in the world. What is a church but a collection of families? If the family is strong, the church is strong.

In 2016, after an evening of prayer in Attawapiskat, we saw a sketch of the layout. There was a large round church in the middle. There were cabin/log house-type buildings around the camp property. These would be utilized year-round during each semester and would be for family lodging. One for each family that is attending the camp. It is important to maintain a sense of family privacy in such a setting.

There will be a general meal hall/kitchen area and other assorted buildings to be used for various training modules. Each building that will be designed and each expansion phase will reflect a key aspect of the Kingdom: excellence.

When we met with the Grand Chief of the Cree, Matthew Coon Come, and his wife in Montreal, we shared with them our heart for the north and what we were seeing in terms of needs. Shortly after this, I asked him if there was a Spirit-filled, faith-first, Bible and missions training centre that he knew of that was in line with what we were seeing. His response to me was clear: "Start one."

While we were in Whitehorse, Yukon Territory, working with the Klinket, God gave me a full Bible school curriculum that could establish a local assembly in the core elements of biblical truth and Kingdom reality in a short duration of time. This will be the core of what is taught. Each course/teaching has been taught and/or preached in the north and south these last three years, proving it out in the real world. The results are clear. It works.

In 2024, during prayer on Pentecost Sunday, Shannon was given the timeframe for the courses and breaks throughout the year, which we've stated above. However, the month off between each training semester will allow us to still travel and connect with various reserves and communities. The need is great, and we are often contacted and asked to come and help in places across Canada, so we know we still need to maintain an aspect of "go ye," as there will be some who simply won't be able to come to where we are. Even Timothy was told to do the work of an evangelist!

Alaya, as she has been so effective in ministering to youth when we've been up north and also has a passion for horses, will be establishing an equine aspect of the camp. Hurting youth can receive ministry as well as explore the peace and comfort of one of God's greatest creatures!

When a family understands that their community is their mission field, they can work with the right attitude to see it won for the Kingdom of God. This is why we see this as essential for the whole family to attend. However, it is true that in some communities, the family that's hungry and committed to work for God may consist of just one person. That is understood, and we will have no barriers to such a situation.

We are simply being obedient to the specific vision of what was shown, as the Holy Spirit has made it clear that the entire family, if possible, is to be trained. Even the little ones? Yes!

Why, just this last time in Wemindji, we saw a wonderful water baptism. Some new believers, and some who had never been baptised, rededicating their lives and following the path of Jesus. However, most of the people that got baptised decided after they saw the first person get baptised, and were subsequently dunked in the clothes they wore to church! And who started this stampede? Why, a young boy, around eleven years old, who decided a few days prior that he needed to get serious about being a Christian. So never underestimate the power of a child! Isaiah 11:6.

The entire vision of the Bible/mission training camp is all in line with a church that can prevail over the gates of Hell (Matthew 16:18) and one that is raised and equipped according to Ephesians 4:11-16, Romans 12:6-8, and 1 Corinthians 12:28.

So this is where we are going. We will continue to visit the communities we have made contact with and reach into new ones, but the mandate is clear: build what the Lord has shown. People from many communities will be able to come to the camp to be trained in a mighty way and then return to their villages to see them won and set free as they walk in the authority and knowledge of Jesus Christ!

Perhaps you are wondering how, or if you could help? Yes! This whole new phase will require much prayer! So please join us, as we are currently praying and seeking God for the right place for the training camp. In everything you build, there are four aspects that must be understood.

1. Doing the right thing.
2. At the right time.
3. In the right way.
4. With the right help.

If you would like to be otherwise involved in this next phase of the ministry, feel free to reach out. God is putting things together for a great push forward these last days. Connecting with effective people in the body of Christ is our great joy, and we have met them all across Canada, from Newfoundland to the Yukon!

Chapter Twenty-Four

The Coming Revival

In James 5:7, we are told that the return of Jesus is directly tied to his waiting for the precious fruit of the earth, and this harvest will not be accomplished until we see an early and latter rain. "*Be patient therefore, brethren, unto the coming of the Lord. Behold, the husbandman waiteth for the precious fruit of the earth and hath long patience for it, until he receive the early and latter rain.*"

This early and latter rain prophetically ties in to Hosea, chapter 6:2-3. "*After two days will he revive us: in the third day he will raise us up, and we shall live in his sight. Then shall we know, if we follow on to know the LORD: his going forth is prepared as the morning; and he shall come unto us as the rain, as the latter and former rain unto the earth.*"

This clearly shows us that there is a harvest that precedes the coming of the Lord and that God Himself is going to help to bring it in by coming "unto us as the rain, as the latter and former rain." With this knowledge, it would only seem fitting that the Holy Spirit would be working on earth to help prepare those who are willing to take part in this great harvest.

Now even though there is a last day's prophetic harvest, it does not change the mandate to the believer to go, teach, lay hands, cast out, etc. You can already go and see thousands saved, healed, and delivered. There is clearly plenty of work for all!

But what we are talking about here is something that no one has yet seen, and that is the grand scale of convicting power God is wanting to unleash.

There are more people on earth today than have ever died in all of history. So without question, God has planned for these days to be a vital focus of His gospel. Jesus said in Matthew 24:14, "And this gospel of the kingdom shall be preached in all the world." He didn't say "a" gospel or some knock-off version. No, the pure, genuine, and mighty gospel shall be preached, directly challenging the kingdom of darkness. Hallelujah!

This is why preparing and equipping the church so that they might effectively co-labour with Christ to bring in the souls that He shed his blood for is so important! Our feet are to be shod with the preparation of the gospel of peace. An army that is prepared is an army that the Lord can use. And those whose hearts are perfect towards him are going to see wonders in these last days that the world has never known, as God Himself will do it! 2 Chronicles 16:9.

This is one of the reasons we've enjoyed our work so much among the First Nations. If you want to find people that can move with the Spirit of God, you've found them. There's so many we've met in all the communities, where no matter how bad the natural situations are, they are hearing and following the voice of the Master and have seen wonderful salvations, healings, and victories of all kinds for years and years. It is a land that brims with testimonies because you need a real God for any success there, and bless the Lord, we have one!

Our role has primarily been to bring strong biblical teaching to whichever community we're in and to deal with some of the spiritual roots and strongholds of evil in the places we go. It's always good to remind the devil he's under our feet.

If we shared the testimonies of everyone we know, this would not be a book but a great volume of reports, filling shelves!

Canada has not been forsaken, for there are surely more than 10 true believers here! Gen 18:32. It's time to expect God! Now is the hour to believe God. Now is the hour to return to your first love. Now is the hour when we might charge the armies of darkness to see scores of salvations, healings, and deliverances among all cultures in Canada, and to such a degree that the cloud of witnesses would wish they were still down here with us, fighting the fight of faith, that we might bring supreme honour and glory to our great and soon-coming King, Jesus!

May God mightily bless you!

For those wanting to connect, give

Or simply reach out.

Please contact us through

www.iamtheway.ca

A special thank you to

Jubilee Stratford
Open Door Christian Fellowship
Shrewsbury Baptist Church
Wild Goose Studio

For your consistent care.

Manufactured by Amazon.ca
Bolton, ON

41660677R00169